The Wheatgrass Mechanism

Don Gayton

The Wheatgrass Mechanism

Science and Imagination in the Western Canadian Landscape

Fifth House Publishers
Saskatoon Saskatchewan

To Buck, Kirwin, and Richard.
Con dignidad.

Canadian Cataloguing in Publication Data
Gayton, Don, 1946-
The wheatgrass mechanism
ISBN 0-920079-70-9
1. Natural history - Prairie Provinces. I. Title.
QH106.2.P6G38 1990 508.712 C90-097141-X

Published with the assistance of The Saskatchewan Arts Board
and The Canada Council.

Cover photograph by Jim Romo.
Map by Bob Fink.
Design: Robert MacDonald, MediaClones Inc.,
Toronto Ontario, Banff Alberta and Saskatoon Saskatchewan.

Versions of "The Grass and the Buffalo," "On the Outlier," and "The Hole
in the Glacier" appeared in *NeWest Review*. "The Hellbender at the
Bottom of the Dugout" appeared in *Briarpatch*. "Deeper into Prairie"
appeared in *Harrowsmith*.

Thanks to Martha Gould of Fifth House for her editorial professionalism
and commitment to this project.

Fifth House Publishers
20 36th Street East
Saskatoon, Saskatchewan S7K 5S8

Printed in Canada

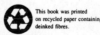

Contents

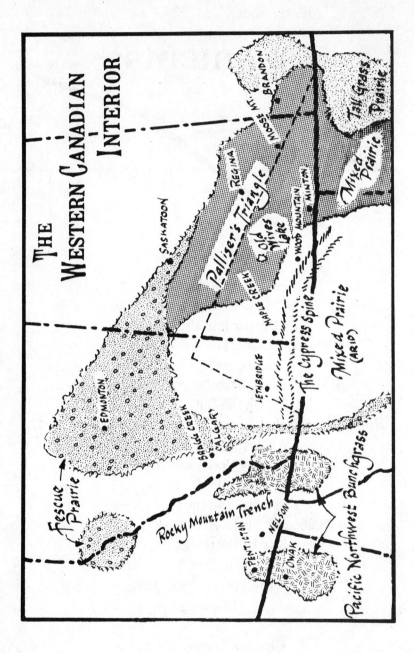

The Western Canadian Interior

Introduction

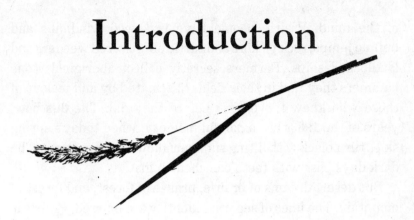

Prairie. The very word seems to suggest broadness. "An expanse of land, of low relief, treeless or nearly so." Brought originally from France, the word prairie is now profoundly North American. To me prairie is a thin membrane of grass, stretched tightly over secret horizons of soil, and shaped by drought, geography, and solitude.

Prairie is one of the great landscapes of interior Western Canada, born and reborn of ancient seas, the Rocky Mountains, and the continental glaciers. Forests lie on its flanks and great rivers have carved through it. It is a region indifferent and often brutal to those who live in it. A love for this region does not come easy; it has been my test case for a larger bond to landscape in general.

Canadian prairie is a bioregion, a crude triangle running from Brandon to Edmonton, down to the foot of the Rockies at the 49th parallel, and back along the border to Brandon again. Wheat is its staggering emperor. This triangle is also a region of the mind. Prairie people have produced windmills and buffalo jumps, rock pickers and turtle effigies, rod weeders and landlocked ships. Farmers secretly collect aboriginal stone hammers they find in their fields, fascinated by and jealous of those who knew the prairie before they did. The dustbowl years of the 1930s are a painful memory; when today's spring skies turn black with lifting summerfallow, few mention it. The dark days pass with teeth clenched on grit.

But desert dreams of prairie, prairie of forest, and forest of mountain. The lines of separate identity are blurred. Prairie is bounded on the south by desert, to the east and north by forests, and to the west by mountains. Borders on all sides are vague and transitory. Within the western mountains lie complex outlier grasslands, and prairies harbor montane scarps and dunes of moving sand. Landscapes and bioregions intergrade, cannot be defined without each other, and desire one another.

The vegetation follows a similar pattern. Draws and coulees have a specific set of prairie vegetation that grades into another set in the saline meadows, another on gravely hilltops, another on lacustrine clays, and another on sand. Change is a dynamic constant, over distance and time.

Buffalo memory persists in the grasses, and they have not yet fully assimilated the cow and the fence. Range managers, now in their middle age, no longer profess such confidence in their understanding of grass and grazer.

Temperatures here can swing through 80 degrees of Celsius, and the violence of summer is tempered only by its brevity. Brutal winters are crowned with momentary aurorae and transcendent sundogs. Average in this country is meaningless; it is a mere summation of profound extremes.

Prairie is also shaped by loss. From these hills of unbroken relict grassland, I can look across to vast stretches of industrialized loam. Native prairie like this becomes a rarity, left unbroken only when it is too steep, too gravely, or too saline. The farmland down below me has been stripped of its landscape; the fields have the sterile elegance of a room with no furniture. In its monotony of monoculture and soil disturbance, our agriculture has little to hold the eye.

Here on this prairie, a modest richness unfolds. I stand near a bison-rubbed rock that is covered with fluorescent lichens. The grasses surrounding it are ancient and silvery. Pussytoes, ground plums, and liatris show off their modest assets, and clubmoss grows across the ground in a standing wave. Where the folding of land holds winter snow, the rose, the buckbrush, and the wolf willow make their appearance.

Native prairies provide the mind with a retreat. Often seen only from a distance, reassuring and private places, they are imagined and recalled more often than actually visited. They become places of composure and personal balance, geographies of hope.

Prairie is also a construct, the idea of a place, one coveted by immigrants and botanists. A destroyer of painters and spawner of writers. All of us come to prairie with notions of what we shall do to it, and the notions work for a while. But in the end the rail lines buckle, dust blows for a decade, and the writers move away. Cautiously, swift foxes reappear, and abandoned grainfields begin their long climb back to the grassland climax.

Prairie, prairie. Graced by crocus, teepee ring and wolf willow. Years of dryness can be broken by a random wet summer, when this thin membrane relaxes. Grasses reach upward. Exotic floral structures develop, and antelope prosper. Junegrass, which in dry years is not seen at all, flowers at a foot high and looks like a crop. Plants gamble everything on the chance the rains will continue. This is a renewal year, one that agronomists try desperately to predict, but prairie simply accepts as its due. Soon enough the membrane will shrink back and turn brittle again. Soon enough these hills and coulees will slide into the pastel indifference of winter, and next summer, who knows? The membrane may again fall under the spell of the Omega Block, a massive dome of dry air that can sit for weeks over this vast landscape.

Prairie, prairie. I kneel right down close to the patterns, rubbing my hand lovingly over a tiny carpet of pussytoes. They are cool and damp, somehow able to coax moisture from this hot and windy afternoon.

The perspective from hands and knees opens up and fills in the prairie. Why should I let a six-foot view of the world tyrannize my vision? Buffalo beans splash a joyful yellow across the green in front of me. Somewhere deep in this plant's leguminous root, profound symbiosis is shared with a bacterium. Up in the air above me, invisible Sprague's pipits trill a single endless, falling song. In the distance, the Trans-Canada Highway rumbles, faint and unimportant. I realize, suddenly, that this is a magic place.

Moving down along the hillside I come to a small, almost bed-sized blowout. Horizontal juniper grows around its edge and the windsifted sand inside is pure and perfect. I step in and carefully lie down, not wanting to disturb anything. A single plant of dropseed, a sand-loving grass, has established itself in the blowout, a minute successional anchor. The continual swirl of wind has caused its stem to trace a circle in the sand, and the tracks of a tiny Ord's kangaroo rat bisect the circle with geometric delicacy.

An angry stinkbug makes its way across my blowout. Its tail is in the air. Stinkbugs always seem to look angry. One of the Saharan species, a cousin to this one, repels predators by spraying hot sulfuric acid from a special chamber in its tail. This one has only its stink and its anger.

I pluck a mature seed of western porcupine grass from the edge of the blowout and moisten its long, twisted awn with my tongue. The awn begins to uncoil, slowly, following internal clocks. Moisture would be the minute hand here, and season the hour. The coiled awn is a lovely mechanism that, at the right hydrological moment, will drill its barbed and sharpened seed into the ground.

The seed and the stinkbug go their separate ways, linked to one another by known and distant relations of diversity and nutrient flow. One can only speculate on linkages not yet known.

This prairie bioregion that surrounds me is also a place where science is practiced, for gain, for need, and occasionally just for the knowledge. Lichen spread on tombstones is used as a benchmark for dating ancient medicine wheels. Synthesized chemical pheromones are wafted in front of moth antennae; any neuronal flutters are watched with great interest. Minute thermocouples are implanted, to explore the mysteries of leaf surface evaporation. Cunning vapor barriers and heat exchangers are developed to conserve heat in winter. Cultivator trip mechanisms and snowmobiles were invented here.

Moving among the scientists engaged in this work, I snatch bits of their technical language so I can handle them and turn them over, like bright and curious objects. And what language! *Geological loading. Feedback inhibition. Gravitrophic movements. Fire disclimax. Edge effects.* What great basins of new metaphor, what ranges for personal exploration! And what solitudes, both chosen and otherwise, that lie just beneath the surface of this language.

There must be a way, beyond condescension, beyond science fiction or simple gee whiz, to open up these territories of science. To analyze them the way a lover studies living flesh.

There may even be other ways of *doing* science as well. The line between imagination and science, between the poem and the technical article, has been very precisely and rigidly drawn. This boundary is so closely guarded that it suggests anachronism, maintained by those whose days of exploration may be over.

Albert Einstein clearly saw the role of imagination in science. His famous "themata" are the biases, personal feelings, and convictions scientists employ as they select observations from the plane of experience in order to create a hypothesis. The second step, testing the hypothesis against reality, is the public, verifiable, and objective part of science, the one we all relate to. Most scientists believe their entire process is objective, but Einstein has placed the first critical step right where it belongs, in the tangled garden of human personality.

Recognizing the role of creativity can be a catharsis for scientists, liberating them into new territories. Conversely, poets might find uses for the null hypothesis or for bar graphs in their work. These aged realms of "science" and "the humanities" hide a very fertile ground at their mutual border, a narrow seam that may someday blossom into a domain itself.

This blowout I sit in is similar in size to the small pits the Blackfoot Indians used to dig. They rimmed the pits with stone and then lay in them until thirst, prairie exposure, and yearning all culminated in a vision. Dream beds, these structures were called, and they can still be found, usually near the top of a high hill in some isolated block of native rangeland. Ranchers and anthropologists come to them secretly, to lie down and imagine.

Stretching out in the warm sand of the blowout, I drop into a light, unencumbered sleep, and the unending, liquid song of the Sprague's pipit comes with me. All else is quiet. History accretes upon itself, the sun advances several degrees, and we move farther into the Holocene.

Waking up a few minutes later, I sense only the residue of a brief prairie dream, but something is different now. Colors have intensified: the green of the horizontal juniper has split into a dozen fine gradations, and the white sand I lie on is dense and textured, like a Mediterranean wall. The sky is inky blue, reverberating as it meets the colors of earth. I wonder if this curious intensity was part of what the Blackfoot looked for.

For years I have walked the landscapes of the western half of this continent, wondering what attracted me to them, but now I think I know. It is the patterns: they are what gives me this overwhelming sense of fulfillment. Architecture of grass and forb and rock and sky. Random patterns. There are a few patterns that I do understand: the layering of buckbrush where winter snowbanks accumulate, the colonization of dry sloughbeds, the frost-heaving of stones. There are a thousand more that I don't understand, in fact, don't even recognize yet as patterns, but there is a pleasant sense of potential. Some patterns may turn out to be truly random assemblages, but most probably will not. Wendell Berry has wondered aloud: Is randomness a verifiable condition, or is it simply a limit of our perception? The most erratic of badland landscapes might actually be reproduced by some complex mathematical fractal.

Somewhere in our cluttered human awareness there is a receptor for these patterns, telling us quietly that they need to be looked upon. This receptor is placed deep in conventional consciousness. It scans for lines of landscape, patterns of rock, assemblages of vegetation. Now that many of these natural patterns are nearly extinct, we begin to see that they do fulfill a basic human need, one that is critical to a sense of peace, and a sense of place.

It is curious how landscapes record in the mind. I find that I carry around a huge library of them. Some are dramatic, like the Pre-Cambrian valley walls of the Frenchman River, the hoodoos of the Alberta Badlands, or the Lizard Range near Cranbrook, but others are not. The thousands of humdrum agricultural fields I have looked at are all there too. The ability to remember landscapes would have been a great survival asset in our nomadic antiquity, and is no doubt coded into our genes. Even though I use the ability now for very different reasons, it is a fine legacy.

So here I am in this landscape of prairie, flush among the patterns that draw me to it. There is the curly profusion of blue grama grass, still green on the dry slope, and barely an inch high. Over here, the seedstalks of porcupine grass, leaning at a characteristic 20 degrees from the vertical, intersecting each other like pick-up sticks. The reddish tinge on the next hillside is a mosaic of the tough and wiry sand reedgrass. To be in these patterns, to revel in them, or even to live in them from afar is natural. To study them is also natural. Patterns cannot be cheapened or destroyed by study; by faint hearts or bad agendas yes, but not by deeper understanding.

The pages that follow are about Western Canada, starting with the prairie landscape and moving westward to link with the Rockies. If I sometimes slip into the frame of reference of "western North America," it is not through any political continentalism, but because geology and vegetation and climate flow freely and gracefully over the 49th parallel. My allegiance is to the landscape, and "Western" is perhaps my only real nationality.

This book is also about plants, myths, dreams, and mechanisms. I like that word, mechanism; the mere mention of it shifts a paradigm, and seems to threaten our intuitive enjoyment of patterns and experience. Artists let themselves be frightened by mechanism, just as scientists shrink from myth, and from imagination. But the worlds of myth and mechanism do finally come together, on the common ground of our natural landscape.

Landscape
Mathematics

Early morning light slowly flooded across a plateau, illuminating first wheatgrass, then sagebrush, then lichen-stained rock. This sunrise was a private showing, held for an 18-year old on a Greyhound walkabout. Ninety-nine dollars for all the prairie the west had to offer. I had gotten off that bus at a late night stop in some distant community (it could have been Eastend, Rifle, Merritt, or Omak) and walked to the edge of town. The few blocks of uncomplicated houses, streetlights and cottonwoods ended abruptly at a three-wire fence and dark, unfathomed space. I crossed over into the blackness, shuffling slowly, and lay down on my bedroll. This was new country, reached at night, and I had no sense of what was around me. But the air was warm and still, and I was glad to be free of the bus for a few hours.

Morning was a revelation. Silence and a cleansing odor of sage enveloped me. A moving curtain of first daylight fired each landscape element in turn with clean, level light. The frayed and blackened trunks of sage were softened by foliage of gray velvet. Coarse mineral soil reflected motes of glassy pink. Rigid seed stalks of nameless grasses strained upward, away from their curving profusions of basal leaves. I turned around to see five spectral antelope, held in the brief and naked moment between curiosity and flight. In the path of advancing sunlight, a distant windmill and watering trough spoke of some lean and minimalist human use of the land. Beyond that lay an enormous mountain-bounded chunk of western space. This was a charmed circle, of parched and improbable beauty.

I plunged deeply into that heart-rending landscape. Back on the bus I wrote letters about it to imaginary women, describing the place as if it were my home, and asking them to join me there. Plains and prairie landscapes, and the small communities they supported, became my passion on that trip, almost a compulsion. I felt the immigrant's urgency at each new place, wanting to embrace the land, to couple upon it, to quickly learn the meaning of its antelope and its burrowing owls, and to understand how livings were made from the brittle bunchgrasses.

Landscape, vision, synaptic firing, memory; the powerful walkabout sequence went on and on. Too long, in the end, when it spilled over the borders of the West to become mere travel, but the memory of grass and sagebrush prairie endured. Years later I redeemed the promise to come back to the region of those persistent images, and settled in to learn from the slow, equinoctial rhythms of an Okanagan cattle ranch.

The headquarters of the Double L lay in a dry glacial valley, surrounded by Ponderosa pine, bluebunch wheatgrass, and rock. This time I was no tourist on the landscape; now I could poke and prod it, explore along its seams, and come back to at it again and again. The irrigated hayfields became my laboratories for plant response, the pastures my observation plots for grazing and recovery, the bluebunch rangeland my magnificent herbarium. I developed a kind of grass kinship, along with a lasting allergy to brome pollen. The Double L offered me the chance to participate in a working anachronism; hired man on an 80-year-old cow-calf outfit that had changed little over the years. This was a job having much to do with landscape, allowing me to fill in some of my prairie images with detail and response. I began to understand the careful and conservative process of making a sustainable grassland living. But all along I knew there was another class of landscape detail, beyond that required for work and wages. After four seasons on the Double L, I finally shifted my focus to the fifth floor of a university library.

Beginning Plant Ecology graduate students were not expected to devote massive blocks of time to library reading, having many other things to attend to, but I became possessed. Journals such as *Planta, Botanical Gazette,* and the *Journal of Range Management* became close companions, and I began to wait impatiently for library staff to shelve the latest issues. Other journals appeared as I summerfallowed through the stacks: *Compost Science,* the *Journal of Irreproducible Results,* and *Aquatic Biology,* among others. All this unsung agony and triumph was found in the labyrinthine shelves of the "Q-to-QK" section.

The pact made with that morning landscape years before had led me to this library, by way of the Double L. Here I found bizarre, almost ritualized views of the same grass and sage-brush: digitized landscapes, creative analogues of function, razor-thin splinters of experience, multiple treatments, and sacred controls. I found all the mystery of a dark Nostradamian heresy, hard by a scientific rigor that verged on the autistic. This was Middle Earth.

I struggled at first with the mere names of my chosen landscape, "prairie," "range," "plain," and "steppe," finding them more evocative than definitive. "Grassland," which evoked little but didn't attempt much either, seemed a useful, functional term. Maps drawn by dogged men like J.E. Weaver showed me how this North American grassland could be divided into provinces. The Northern Great Plains province takes in a vast swath of western Canada, the Dakotas, and eastern Montana, plus a part of Colorado and Nebraska. Continuing southward into Texas and northeastern Mexico are the Southern Plains grasslands. The valleys of the Rockies and other ranges of the west coast hold the dry and narrow Pacific Northwest Grasslands; to the south of them, in Nevada and Utah, are the Great Basin Desert Grasslands. Each of these provinces is subdivided into a patchwork quilt of subtypes based on the dominant vegetation.

Our northern prairies are relatively young landscapes, developing after the last late Pleistocene glaciers retreated and the southern forests collapsed in the face of increasing drought. The grassy vegetation that colonized this vast new niche did not evolve in place. Instead, forest understory grasses slowly speciated outward from the eastern and northern fringes on to the new land, honing new mechanisms of survival as they spread.

Native grasslands also form the matrix of what western identity we have, since they are only found west of a line drawn through Manitoba and down along the Mississippi River to the Gulf. The grasslands have produced a style of dress, a traditional literature and an emerging one, a sense of political alienation, and a sense of individual independence. Somewhere, in the dense overlay of political boundaries and administrative divisions, lies a thin and shadowy republic of prairie.

Climatologists can define prairie as simply a level, unprotected region where evaporation through the growing season slightly exceeds incoming rainfall. On our prairies, that differential is created by the powerful rainshadow effect of British Columbia's mountains. They force the great inbound masses of moisture-laden Pacific air upward, extracting their moisture in the process. By the time these air masses drop exhausted down the eastern foothills, they are bone dry. The exposure and dryness during the growing season discourages trees and favors shrubs and grasses that have tough, minimalist aboveground structures, and massive root systems.

Fire is another creator of grasslands, killing woody trees and shrubs that have aboveground growing points and sparing grasses, which regrow from ground level. Man has always been a creature of grasslands and savannah, and his presence in North America is probably intimately linked to fires and the maintenance of grasslands. If fire did not start naturally, then humans probably set periodic fires, for reasons that are interesting to speculate on.

At some point early in this century man's commitment to the use of fire reversed itself, and modern fire suppression has led to massive forest ingrowth into traditional grasslands, notably along the Rocky Mountain Trench. Our society will eventually have to come to terms with the rejuvenating power of fire in the landscape. Since fire comes inevitably to forest/grassland interfaces, occasional small fires, intentionally set, may be preferable to storing fuel indefinitely for the inevitable large wildfire.

Most days I worked at the same large corner table on the fifth floor of the library. The table was also used by a very elegant older woman who was doing a doctoral thesis on the Irish playwright J.M. Synge. We shared an enthusiasm for primary sources, and occasionally we used each other as cross-disciplinary sounding boards. If I could give her a clear and enthusiastic summary of my day's reading, or vice versa, that was a good sign.

Through the narrow windows of the library I could see a fairsized chunk of the Canadian prairies, and that view was a good reminder of the place-context of my studies. This was no fecund, temperate birthplace of plant research, like England's Rothamstead, Holland's Wageningen or Maryland's Beltsville: this was a cold, near-desert of short, violent summers and murderous winters. Captain John Palliser once declared most of it not suitable for habitation by Europeans.

I found out early on in my studies that many of the sophisticated plant mechanisms and symbioses described in the research journals did not operate here. What I found instead were multiple systems of endurance and individual survival. Western wheatgrass, for example, produces tiny wax plates on its leaf surfaces to help seal off water loss. The leaf is deeply ribbed, like a piece of corrugated cardboard, and its stomata are nested in the recesses between ribs. Under drought stress, the leaf edges will curl upward to form a long narrow tube, still allowing the leaf to function but reducing drought exposure. Most of the stomata of western wheatgrass leaves are on the upper side, so the leaf can continue atmospheric transactions within the protected space of the tube. The plant reproduces by extending rhizomes outward in the relative protection of the soil, rather than risking seed production aboveground in the ever present summer sun.

To imagine endless seasons passing over a stand of western wheatgrass, and the slow accretion of these mechanisms into genetic identity, is to glimpse a very fundamental prairie timeline.

Most of the grasses and forbs on this dry prairie flower early, I discovered. They shoehorn their life cycle into the generally cooler, wetter months of April, May, and June. The rest of the season is devoted to the slow building up of food reserves for the winter, until frost draws a curtain on the growth period in late September or October. Then the prairie juggernaut – winter – arrives, bringing wind, precious little snow, and paralyzing temperatures.

Botanist Jan Looman puzzled over the distribution of the so-called "warm-season" grasses, the C4 species that make up the tallgrass prairie. Why were they only found on the very eastern edge of the prairies, when summers on the western side were just as warm, if not warmer? Looman studied the problem and proposed the following answer: warm-season dropseed and bluestem grasses flower in late June and July, at least a month later than the cool season wheatgrasses and stipas, and they must have sufficient midsummer moisture to complete their life cycle. He found that by mapping spring/summer precipitation ratios across the prairies, he could predict the location of warm-season grasses wherever summer rainfall was greater than spring rainfall. Looman's theory fit over the biogeographical reality quite well: those regions that historically supported tallgrass vegetation had summer precipitation at least equal to, if not greater than, spring precipitation.

Winter is the next hurdle. January on the prairie will usually deliver at least a few days that approach minus 40, but oddly enough, the critical period for the survival of a prairie plant is not those arctic mornings, but early spring. April is a month when winter and summer can splice deeply into one another, with devastating results for plants as they green up. Regina weather in the spring of 1981 was a typical example. Daytime highs for the first 12 days of April of that year were well above freezing at 7, 12, even as high as 17 degrees celsius. Lows were modest, averaging around minus 3. Then, on the 13th, a cold front moved in, and the daytime high reached only one degree celsius. That night the mercury dropped to minus 13. The next day was clear and calm, allowing the temperature to soar to 24 degrees. The night of the 15th the temperature dropped again to minus 6.

For many cultivated plants that had survived the previous winter, April 1981 was the last straw. Yet the great bulk of native grasses do survive the roughest of prairie winters and springs, a remarkable feat of thermal stress engineering.

A slight excess of evaporation over precipitation creates grassland. A greater excess, as in the case of British Columbia's Okanagan valley, results in a desert grassland. There, plant surface areas contract even more and diameters increase, as in the sagebrush, bitterbrush and cactus. Roots of the scrubby Ponderosa pine explore deeply into gravel and rock outcroppings. Opportunist species like the annual cheatgrasses race through brief life cycles in the few precious days of wet spring.

Climatology is a fascinating prism for viewing and defining landscape and ecotype. The concept of water balance is clear and intuitive. But more personal, more synaptic visions of Canadian prairie abound that are equally elegant. Here is one the library produced, from the Irish adventurer William Butler, writing in the 1870s:

"But [this] ocean is one of grass, and the shores are the crests of mountain ranges, and the dark pine forests of the sub-Arctic regions. The great ocean itself does not present more infinite variety than does this prairie-ocean of which we speak. In winter, a dazzling surface of the purest snow; in early summer, a vast expanse of grass and pale pink roses; in autumn too often a wild sea of raging fire. No ocean of water in the world can vie with its gorgeous sunsets; no solitude can equal the loneliness of night-shadowed prairie ..."

The North American prairie has been ravaged. Between plowing and overgrazing, it is perhaps the most extensively altered biome on the planet, and we know very little of its original ecology and function. Thus the historical observations by Butler and others – who saw this land in an essentially virgin state – become tremendously important to contemporary students of this landscape and its resources. "We don't know what we're doing because we don't know what we've undone," is Wendell Berry's commentary on prairie agriculture.

A new discipline must be forged – historical ecology – that will reconstruct the evolution of western North American landscape from the Late Pleistocene to about 1950. Outrageously diverse sources would be consulted in building this discipline: pollen rain in lake sediments, radiocarbon bone analysis, glacial air-bubble sampling, aboriginal legends, and explorer's journals. This would not be the recovery of an existing history, but the synthesis of a new one.

I have daydreamed of commanding William Butler off his horse, down onto his knees amid the dusty grass and roses, to tell me exactly what he sees. Lovely poetry Bill, but now I want you to give me details about species composition, percent cover, buffalo grazing patterns, rates of litterfall, fire frequency, and soil microbial populations. As a matter of fact, sit down, Bill, this may take a while.

For a long time I was transfixed at that fifth floor library table, using the window at my elbow as a reference point, and reading prairie. Plant physiology and plant ecology gradually emerged as my specialties, my favored prisms of view. The memory of that distant morning landscape did not become a faded photograph from another time; it simply shifted from simple experience to part of my identity.

When I look back on that walkabout I realize that love is hopelessly entangled in our landscape equations. We see new country as a conjugal garden, or occasionally as a boundless plain for cowboy solitude and misogyny. We have a recurring need to commit ourselves, and the western landscape is always available. What a spectacular host for that commitment.

The entanglement of the factors of landscape and love has given us a culture of the West, an urgency, and a closeness to the earth. But somewhere in one of the parent equations is another factor for tearing down and remaking landscape. This factor, by which we hope to provide for those loved ones and prove something to them, is the virus that is slowly destroying the whole mathematics.

There is a famous photograph by Ansel Adams called "Moonrise over Hernandez, New Mexico" that shows a tiny community of adobe houses and ancient cottonwoods, set in a vast layered landscape of dry riverbed and desert, with the Sangre de Cristo mountain range in the distance. A print of that photograph hangs on the wall of my study. I think Hernandez may represent, in spite of its rural stasis and Hispanic contradiction, one of the finest sustainable relations between man and land that North America has yet produced. The Hernandez human community expressed great passion and empathy for its landscape and revised it very little, probably paying a price in its lack of material progress. Adams, who worked in natural landscapes almost exclusively, must have felt there was something special about this village, something very harmonious about its landscape equation, in order to include it in his portfolio.

Hernandez is not a dream: it actually exists, produced as a conscious choice by its inhabitants, the same way Calgary and Trail are produced. I hope we can someday rewrite our own landscape mathematics to include some small fraction of the Hernandez factor.

In the Heart of the Matter: Phloem Research

No one had ever seen living plant phloem in action before, but James Small had come very close. To expose the operation of that complex and minute circulation system had become a passion for him over the years. Small worked alone, developing a surgical excision method that, because of its sheer delicacy, he knew would never become a standard technique. But when you are that close, you don't quit.

In 1936, Small set up for a final attempt, one that incorporated several new modifications to his technique. He planted a special variety of squash in the greenhouse, one that did well indoors and had a large, succulent stem. Then he made an exhaustive search for the best cutting instruments he could find, eventually selecting very sharp German scalpels used for eye surgery. To prepare, Small laid a live squash stem across his microscope stage and cut a thin, longitudinal slice from it. Slowly, with glacial calm, he shaved away slice after slice from the upper and lower sides of the stem until there was only a paper thin – but intact – strip of stem tissue remaining. He hoped that it was thin enough to transmit light but thick enough to contain a few uncut, functioning phloem strands. Small then flooded the exposed tissue with water and leaned back for a moment to calm any remaining tremors. This was it. He switched on the powerful microscope lamp and focused.

His eye followed the familiar landscape as it went from cottony vagueness to clear detail. The elongated, spliced phloem cells appeared, but all were cut or damaged in some way. Patiently, the scientist shifted to another part of the cut stem, and began another methodical scan. Over the years he had developed a very fluid and precise microscope technique; the instrument disappeared, and it was Small himself that glided through layer after layer of cell.

Something caught his eye. There, out at the margin, was a suggestion of movement. Small went over to it and saw immediately that it was an intact phloem strand. His own circulation system began to race as he watched, fascinated. The limpid contents of each cell, the stuff of vegetable life, swirled in a slow, clockwise motion. Tiny bits of material, big enough to create circular distortions of light but too small to be seen, rode on the stately currents. He thought immediately of galaxies.

* * *

Phloem is a mechanism of landscape; it is the heart, vessel and living sap of all regional floras. A journey toward understanding forest, desert, grassland or wetland must ultimately pass through phloem. The great field ecologists who first defined vegetation associations had trouble accepting the knowledge of physiologists like James Small, who came equipped with lab coats, and were forever talking about enzymes and cellular systems. But both eventually recognized the usefulness of the other's discipline, and physiological ecology was born.

The Matador Grassland, a huge chunk of native prairie in west central Saskatchewan, was the site of one of these early collaborations. Field ecologists who had surveyed the Matador were asked to choose a suitable site for the physiologists. The ecologists cast their measurements in the four directions, finally choosing a tiny, quarter-meter-squared area that they claimed was a true representative of the northern wheatgrass/ western wheatgrass association found at Matador. The physiologists, awkward and still dressed in lab coats, dragged a host of analytical equipment to the site, gently lowered a specially designed, transparent, ventilated bubble over the chosen spot, and began to take some of the first measurements of carbon flow in working prairie. That was in the 1970s; the results still provoke argument.

Vegetation can really be described as nicely packaged bundles of phloem and xylem. An architecture of plumbing, thinly coated with chlorophyll. Plants move an extensive trade of liquids and nutrients across membranes, down gradients of concentration, and through changes of physical state. Their vast networks of roots silently probe the soil mass in search of water. Their leaves absorb huge quantities of sunlight for photosynthesis, but are kept cool by a water-based evaporative cooling system. (The first phases of nutrient uptake are dovetailed into this cooling system.) Herbaceous and succulent plants derive their structural strength from cells that are pressurized with liquid. Certain saline-adapted plants can actually absorb saline water, separate the salts and then excrete them before they reach toxic levels.

All of these functions are handled by the plant vascular system – the plumbing. The two networks of the vascular system are xylem and phloem, terms that can provoke allergic reactions in those with unpleasant memories of Botany 100. To clarify, xylem transports water extracted from the soil, and phloem transports the sap plants produce for their own further growth. (The two systems can be kept separate by a phonetic memory device – phloem transports phood.)

Xylem function is fairly well understood. However, despite the discoveries of James Small and others, the way the phloem works is still essentially unsolved.

Results of phloem transport are readily seen. The main stem of northern wheatgrass exports its nutrients through phloem to nourish new shoots, or tillers. Fireweed matures from the bottom up, and the dying lower leaves export their nutrients through the phloem, up to developing seeds. Quackgrass sends its insidious rhizomes into our gardens, fueled by energy produced by the parent plant over in the neighbor's yard. We can demonstrate these phloem movements by injecting a marker compound into the system in one part of the plant and detecting it somewhere else.

Just exactly *how* materials move in the phloem is another question. The discipline of plant physiology goes back ten generations and now has to its credit a nearly complete understanding of mechanisms like photosynthesis, seed germination, and cell initiation. Thus it is not surprising that the unsolved problem of phloem transport has attracted to it some of the most creative minds in the discipline. An elaborate, purposeful and unknown mechanism is very compelling to certain scientific personalities.

Research on phloem has been vastly complicated by an automatic wounding reaction that activates whenever a strand is punctured. This mechanism – strikingly similar to the mammalian mechanism of blood clotting – automatically fills the cut phloem with a bulky substance that brings activity in that line of cells to a sudden and complete stop. Sap clotting is almost universal in plants. It is interesting to note that two exceptions to this clotting rule – the sugar maple and the rubber tree – are exploited commercially for their phloem sap.

To add to the set of difficulties, it is nearly impossible to isolate phloem without damage. Tiny, single-celled strands wander through massive xylem and stem tissues. Small was the only scientist with the patience and ability to physically isolate phloem strands without damage, and his technique died with him.

In contrast to James Small's approach, an alternate tactic of phloem researchers was to cut the system open, watch how it operated for a few seconds as it collapsed, and make guesses about how it worked under more normal circumstances. Plant physiologists do admire elegance though, and this method never became a standard in the discipline either.

Physiological tracing is a technique that did meet the test of elegance. Tracers are chemicals of powerful recognition, even in minute quantities, that can be injected into plants and recovered. Because of its similarity to natural plant constituents, the plant is fooled into handling the tracer normally. Plant physiologists had the honor of developing this concept and presenting it to fellow biologists and ecologists.

Fluorescent dyes were the first tracers to be used. As far back as the 1880s, physiologists were injecting small quantities of these dyes into functioning phloem at one site, and recovering them at another. But the dyes were not without their problems. Plants were found to be full of their own fluorescent compounds, which confused the detection of tracers. Worse yet, the most successful of the tracer dyes were also potent growth hormones, which radically altered the growth of an injected plant.

Fluorescent tracer work persisted, in the absence of better methods, until the advent of radioactive isotope tracers during World War II. Tracer deception then moved from the level of the molecule to the level of the electron. Among the everyday chemical groceries that plants take up, researchers would slip in a few bogus radioactive atoms that differed from the real ones by the width of Avogadro's eyelash. Yet this difference was enough for the powerful geiger counters to sense, and a new methodology was born. J.W. Spinks of the University of Saskatchewan is commonly credited with the first use of radioactive tracers in plants in 1946, but the actual pioneer, as far as I can tell, was a Washington State University botanist named Orlin Biddulph, who used radioactive phosphorous in bean plant investigations in 1943.

In spite of the elegance of the radiotracer deception, even this method has been called into question. We now find that plants do discriminate between certain normal and radioactive isotopes, and treat them differently. It is really remarkable that phloem researchers have not all turned to drywalling for a living.

Plant physiologists have wrestled elegantly with their difficult discipline, and have often achieved quantum advances by borrowing techniques from other fields. The aphid stylet technique is a case in point.

In 1953 a minor technical note was published in *Science* magazine by the entomologists Kennedy and Mittler, describing a new method for studying aphid feeding habits. Aphids are so lazy they don't even suck plant sap: they simply puncture the phloem with a minute feeding tube and let the hydraulic pressure in the phloem force the sap into their guts. The two entomologists discovered that by anaesthetizing aphids while they were feeding and then clipping their bodies off, phloem sap would continue to bleed out through the cut feeding tube that remained. The entomologists were then able to analyze exactly what the aphids were getting in their diet.

This was a small advance for bug men, but a great breakthrough for phloem investigators. Messrs. Weatherly and Peel, plant physiologists of eclectic reading habits, immediately saw that the lowly aphid could provide them with a very precise investigative tool. The insects not only penetrated the phloem without triggering callose formation, they also entered only one strand at a time, and studiously avoided any nearby xylem strands. Weatherly and his colleagues now had a method for sampling functional, uninterrupted phloem. Aphids had figured out the recondite architecture of the plant circulation system, and the physiologists could use them as expendable tour guides. A massive bug slaughter ensued.

Several highly significant experiments were performed using this technique, including a lovely "experimentum crucis" by Weatherly and Peel, proving simultaneous bi-directional movement of materials in a single phloem strand, a physiological mind-blower. Weatherly and Peel's paper describing the experiment is a treat to read. The materials and methods section of the paper details the use of fluorescent dyes, radioactively labeled carbon dioxide, time charts, and aphid stylets.

The terse scientific descriptions barely conceal the creative imagination that went into the work.

Weatherley and Peel also proved that plants have ionic "pumps" and are able to maintain a positive pressure in the phloem sufficient to force sap out of the aphid stylet.

Armed with the stylet technique, phloem researchers press on, chipping away at the fine structure of phloem cells and the actual mechanisms of solute movement. The electron microscope is a great help. Because the problem has been so resistant to solution, research on it goes far beyond the conventional level of speculation and creativity. This great gap in our knowledge of plants will continue to irritate plant scientists until one of them solves it. That someone will likely be bored and dissatisfied by the usual statement of the problem and conventional research on it. He or she may turn briefly to reading about bridge engineering for mental refreshment, perhaps just long enough to see the flash of insight leading to a breakthrough in approach or technique.

The final illumination of plant vascular complexity will be quite an event, celebrated and envied by laboratories around the world. After the hoopla dies down we will see the first tentative work testing the new knowledge in real, outdoor conditions. Laboratory researchers will stand awkwardly in the bright sun, and field ecologists will mutter under their collective breath. But together they will be adding another facet to the prism through which we look at landscape.

Deeper Into Prairie

Wind sifts over an undulating, directionless sea of hills, a rare block of original prairie. The outright greens of spring have given way to midsummer bluegreens, yellows and browns. Here, on top of one of the higher hills, is a circle of stones, with a firepit still visible in the center. Anthropologist John Dormaar found two teepee ring sizes on the prairies: a smaller one that predates the arrival of the horse, and a larger one that came after. This looks to be one of the large ones.

Surely there were practical reasons why plains Indians made their camps on hilltops like this one. The movements of people and game could be seen from a distance, stronger winds would keep the mosquitoes down, and so on. But there may also have been spiritual reasons for exposing oneself to a great sweep of distance. A culture that needed dream beds may have also needed this calm and oceanic view.

Prairie can be so large and featureless from this perspective that it ceases to be a landscape at all. It becomes tangible only at a microscopic, hands-and-knees level. From a distance prairie is an abstract. Clouds fill in, as does the mind.

Underneath this teepee ring is a soilscape, with strata of deposition, lenses of gravel, and columns of solonetz. An opaque mirror of the sky, soil also contains random shapes and elegant bands of color. Both sky and soilscapes change unpredictably.

Those who study the soils of this country make direct connections between their medium and the sky when they dig test holes. Sunlight is necessary to fully appraise soil colors, so in the morning the soil surveyor stands to the southeast as he digs a test hole, keeping the sun over his shoulder, and he slowly shifts around to the southwest as the day wears on. The reward for hours of shovel work is the unexpectedly rich blacks of litter, the browns of organic staining, and the mineral yellows.

Color has such a profound meaning in soil that it forms the basis of the four great taxonomic groups of Western Canadian soil science: the Browns, Dark Browns, Blacks and Grays. Hans Jenny, the famous soil classification expert, took a year off late in his career to study color through the medium of painting. Prairie potters seek out these subtle colors of earth in clays from places like Eastend, Lethbridge, Wood Mountain.

Then there are the sands. There is something special about sandy soils. They blow, they reach phenomenally high surface temperatures, they hold virtually no water and fewer nutrients. Yet sands support the most diverse native plant communities on the prairies. The desert sands of the southwestern United States and Mexico support the most diverse plant communities of North America.

There is a little elevator town, Ernfold, that sits on shallow, gravely soil on the CPR Main Line between Moose Jaw and Swift Current. The remarkable thing about Ernfold, visible from miles away, is the single row of blue spruce. Towering over the prairie, the tallest trees in the whole region, the mature and majestic spruces follow the CP tracks on either side of Ernfold. Like Tom Sukanen's landlocked ship at Beechy, they are anomalies on the landscape. Legend has it that the trees were planted back in the 'teens by a local railroad section hand. No one is there to care for them now, section crews having left Ernfold long ago. But the spruces are content. They were planted along a high, sandy ridge, and got a helping hand through the seedling stage. That was all the trees needed. Even though they may never reproduce, life to a full term is assured. They might even outlive Ernfold.

Sandy soils seem to be the only prairie soils that permit a healthy growth of conifers. The heavier loams and clay loams common to the area may heave and buckle in the spring, refuse to allow hardening off in the fall, create oxygen shortages around the roots, or allow the pH to rise too high for conifers. No one really knows the reason. But fir, spruce, pine, larch and cedar, so sought after by both urban and rural landscapers, frequently die protracted, malingering deaths on the prairies, unless they are in sand.

Soil of any kind is a curious and difficult medium. It is scientifically and economically important, like space, or the oceans. It can be approached through physics, chemistry, geography, microbiology, geology, or rarely, art. But soil is opaque, and agonizingly random. You begin to see the reasons why soil science is not a familiar discipline, and why it is well known for attracting unique and difficult personalities.

Soil was once thought to be non-living matter. Now we know that nearly every characteristic of soil is affected by living organisms. Nostoc, for example, is an insignificant-looking blackish algae crust frequently seen on bare patches of soil. It has been found to contribute to the soil nitrogen economy by fixing atmospheric nitrogen.

Then there are the huge and rapidly cycling populations of soil microorganisms that break down plant litter. Live bacteria, dead bacteria, fungi, microbial waste products, and free enzymes of microbial origin are components of nearly all soils. A common rule of thumb is that each gram of agricultural soil will contain roughly 1,000,000,000 separate microorganisms.

One microbiologist, trying desperately to get around the problem of opacity while estimating the size of soil microbial populations, hit on an indirect but revelatory method. He took the biological energy compound ATP as an analogue of live soil microbial biomass. ATP is a good measure, since it is present in all living organisms and breaks down rapidly after death. Fireflies also use ATP to run their tiny phosphorescent lanterns. The microbiologist leached ATP from a soil sample and added it to an extract of firefly tails. The amount of phosphorescence produced was a measure of the size of the soil microbial population: the greater the glow, the more microbes present in the soil. This is a bioassay in the truest sense of the word, developed by a scientist who was thinking right at the level of the organism.

Occasionally these microbes make themselves manifest. The wanderer of prairie might stumble onto a puffball, a curious leathery sphere the size of a large egg. At some obscure signal, miles and miles of underground fungal threads will join to form this curious reproductive structure (the Spanish name for it is "witch's fart"). Once the puffball breaks open, wind will carry its spores for miles.

Other soil dwellers make their mark. The classic prairie chernozems – the most highly developed of all the grassland soils – can become literally saturated with the introduced earthworm. Researchers are divided on the value of this immigrant from the Old World: earthworms aerate soils effectively with their tunnels, but they also break down huge quantities of stable organic matter and convert it to less stable forms. Viruses, springtails and nematodes are also part of the prairie soil bestiary.

The tallgrass prairies that once grew on these chernozem soils are history. When early explorers wrote home about stirrup-high grasses, they were talking about the bluestems of the tallgrass prairie which covered the eastern Dakotas, reaching up across the southern borders of Manitoba and Saskatchewan. Modern students of plant ecology often have difficulty with the concept of tallgrass prairie because there is simply none of it left. The prodigious fertility of the chernozem underneath was its undoing.

Beneath this teepee ring is another scape, the prehistoric one: scattered thinly across this land are dinosaur beds, medicine wheels, fossilized trees, ancient kill sites, glacial flutings, and strange concretions. Artifacts of a past so distant that memory no longer has a place. Deduction and imagination thus become powerful tools.

A certain response to the prairie grass and wind and stars once inspired the construction of elaborate stone medicine wheels, such as the one at Moose Mountain, Saskatchewan. To the builders, it was clear then why the long strings of rock needed to radiate from the center cairn at precise angles, why the wheels faced the sky, and to whom they spoke. Some archaeologists speculate that medicine wheels were used for astronomical observations, to help mark the course of the seasons. Others feel they were more ceremonial in nature. No one knows for sure. Momentarily clearing the mind of the conventional, expected realities, and standing among the modern grass and wind and stars, the reasons for the medicine wheels may become clear again.

The stones of my teepee ring weather quietly. There were once thousands of rings, wheels, pictographs, and boulder effigies on the prairies: now we are left with a few hundred at most. The rest were victims of our continuing need to consume land.

These stone structures are a mute reminder of a shifting but metastable occupation of this land that goes back some 10,000 years, and may someday be found to go back 50,000 years, to the late Pleistocene. This period, the era before the present one, created the prairie landscape and set the basic terms for human use of it. There was a time during that era when humans coexisted with sabertooth tiger, mastodon, and superbison. The late Pleistocene history of the prairies is foggy and obscure. Yet there may be landscape lessons behind that fog that would have great meaning for today.

The Cree, Blackfoot, Sioux, Sarcee, Gros Ventre, Saulteaux, Assiniboine, and Metis cultures were all nearly extinguished by European colonization of the Canadian prairies. That colonization process was certainly less brutal than an earlier one in the United States, but the net effect was the much the same. The colonial society, with its overwhelming sense of cultural superiority, effectively denied the histories of these aboriginal cultures, rendering them all but invisible. But bits and pieces of those histories do come to light, and two very significant fragments are from the region of Wood Mountain, Saskatchewan.

Sitting Bull and his band lived in the hills just south of Wood Mountain from 1876 to 1881. They came seeking refuge after their unprecedented rout of the U.S. Cavalry at Little Bighorn. To the credit of the Dominion Government of the day, they were allowed to stay, safe from military reprisals. But time, the death of the buffalo herds, and hunger took their toll. Dominion officials allowed the Sioux to enter Canada, but never offered citizenship or material assistance, for fear of angering the Americans. One Canadian, R.C.M.P. Major James Walsh, took a personal interest in the well-being of the Sioux. However, when word of this got back to Ottawa, Walsh was quickly transferred away from Wood Mountain.

Sitting Bull watched his band slowly disintegrate from hunger, disease, and internal strife, and finally gave in to the persistent demands for his return to American soil. He knew full well what would happen once he went back, and resigned himself to it. In 1890 he was murdered by reservation officials in Standing Rock, North Dakota. That was the end of an era.

A few of Sitting Bull's younger generals refused to return, and stayed on at Wood Mountain. Long Dog, one of the Chief's most trusted associates, is buried there. Andrew Ferguson, a contemporary Sioux rancher from Wood Mountain, showed me the gravesite, an isolated bluff on the reserve. There is a simple metal marker and a rough wooden fence. There is no mowed lawn, just the native stipas and wheatgrasses.

That tiny graveyard at Wood Mountain links us to another luminary in North American aboriginal history. Many historians feel that Chief Joseph was the greatest military mind the continent ever produced, better than either Sitting Bull or Robert E. Lee.

Joseph's crime was an attempt to return to the eastern Oregon hill country that was taken from his people, the Nez Percé. The U.S. cavalry went after the band, and in what was probably the first example of guerrilla warfare, Joseph and his people alternately eluded the troops and struck them unexpectedly. The action lasted for most of 1879 and ranged through Oregon, Idaho and Montana. But the inevitable end could be postponed only so long, Joseph knew, as did Sitting Bull before him. After an agonizing powwow in eastern Montana, Joseph gave himself up. The authorities resettled Joseph and his followers in Nespelem, a dreary community in northeastern Washington, cruelly close to their beloved Wallowa country. Joseph wrapped himself in his blanket and waited to die.

But a few of his people did not. Living on leather and exhaustion, they slipped across the Medicine Line into Saskatchewan, becoming part of the ethnic mix that is Wood Mountain. One of the immigrants was White Bird. Another small metal plate marks his resting place in that legendary graveyard.

The wind across this hilltop is a steady pressure, combing through the grass and the teepee ring. This is the wind that blows empty grain bins into the coulees and turns snow into polished marble. In the old days it carried mosquitoes away from hilltop Indian encampments. Now, in dry years, it carries away the summerfallow. In prairie cities, still imperfectly tuned to their environment, it tips over park benches and destroys young garden transplants. Lethbridge, on the dry prairies of southeastern Alberta, has an average windspeed of 20 kilometers per hour, day and night, winter and summer. It is a fact of this bioregion, like winter, grasshoppers, and the CPR.

Teepee rings, dream beds, buffalo jumps, turtle effigies. Marks on the land: myths. These things are not found on farmland, only on the dwindled remnants of native prairie, along with the burrowing owl, the crocus, and the horned toad. The symbols and essences of our natural bioregion are slowly being traded off in our dubious quest to be the world's breadbasket. Somehow we must find room for both the natural essences and the wheat. They need each other.

Salt of
the Earth

In the spring of 1988, North America's fourth largest saline waterbody, Old Wives Lake, dried up. The exposed lakebed, encompassing some 300 square kilometers of southern Saskatchewan, was a vast new surface of very fine brownish silt, mixed with equally fine crystals of sodium sulfate. By June, it had begun to blow.

Greasy clouds of thermonuclear proportions boiled up out of Old Wives, moving southeast along the prevailing summer windtrack. Cattle in downwind pastures sickened, and drought-stunted grain crops were further damaged by the salty deposits.

Oldtimers were divided on whether or not the lake had fully disappeared in the drought of the 1930s. Few people visit the isolated lake, and you can never really tell if what you see in the distance is water or a mirage. There was no agreement either on why Old Wives was drying up. Wood River, the lake's only water source, lost some water to a recent wildlife diversion, but quick calculations showed that regaining the diverted water would have postponed the inevitable by only a week or so. A shift in weather patterns, excessive summerfallow in the region, a cycle of dry years, slough drainage, the greenhouse effect: all were possible causes, but very hard to pin down.

By July, Old Wives and the salty dust clouds had broken into the local television news. Government was called in to deal with the growing problem. After weeks of intense study, engineers emerged with a proposal to drill a deep well nearby and pump water back into the lakebed to stop soil drifting.

Further meetings were scheduled. The media soon lost interest, and the virtually rainless summer of 1988 wore on. The Old Wives district slowly settled back to the gritty obscurity it was used to.

The drying up of Old Wives was a politician's nightmare, a random natural event of uncertain cause, and without obvious solution. The legislators must have thought grimly of the Old Wives' legend, in which a marauding party of Blackfoot was tricked into thinking that a series of nighttime bonfires tended by a few old wives was a huge Cree encampment. But to a plant ecologist, the Old Wives event was a rare opportunity. The receding waters had exposed a brand new and absolutely empty niche. Watching that niche could provide a capsule view, an accelerated microcosm, of a cooling, juvenile earth and the beginning of life.

Niche is not unique to places like Old Wives; niches are everywhere, but simpler to see in new environments. The idea of niche is perhaps the fundamental concept of ecology; it is the multidimensional space that a plant (or any other living organism) fills. Niche can be thought of as the abstract address at the intersection of a hundred biophysical streets. Temperature, sunlight, nutrients, and water are the big boulevards of niche. Backstreets of soil texture, snow cover, and salinity are then further crisscrossed by smaller alleys and pathways of selenium content, insect predation, wind levels during pollination, and so on. A plant's tolerances and capabilities in the biophysical environment will give it either a wide or narrow address in the infinite neighborhood of niche.

There are nearly always neighbors alongside the niche address occupied by a given plant. Some neighbors separate themselves into an overstory, or displace themselves temporally by growing very early or very late in the season. Others are quite willing to compete directly for the niche.

Most of the traditional chemical herbicide industry is based on ignorance of the ecological niche concept. These chemical "silver bullets" kill undesirable plants all right, sometimes whole fields of them, but they do not destroy the niche. Unless other, more desirable plants are primed and ready to spring immediately into the empty niche, a new flush of weeds will simply occupy it again.

A new niche, such as the Old Wives' lakebed, can be a laboratory for natural plant succession, from earliest pioneer species up to stable climax. What made the Old Wives' niche particularly interesting was the presence of adequate below-ground moisture, heavy clay soil, surface drifting, and tremendously high soil salinity. The very toughest of agricultural crops will tolerate up to 12-14 units of salinity; the surface of Old Wives' lakebed came in at around 90. All three hundred square kilometers of it.

Water, nutrients and salinity are so closely intertwined that functionally they can be a single ecological boulevard leading to niche. Nutrients do not move without water; a whole bag of dry fertilizer is useless to a plant without water to dissolve it and move it to the roots. And salinity is simply an excess of certain nutrients. Calcium, for instance, is an essential plant nutrient, but soil calcium in excess is salinity, with all its attendant difficulties.

The foundation of plant water and nutrient uptake begins with a root probing the soil. This root is "blind": it cannot sense water from a distance and grow toward it. Its growth, however, is tremendously responsive to water: a randomly growing root that stumbles into a moist area will experience more rapid growth than its drier neighbors. If that root passes through the moist area back into dry soil, tip growth will again slow down, but the part of the root still in the moist area will begin to branch extensively.

Roots then draw soil moisture, this complex, earthy soup of dissolved chemicals, into themselves through microscopic root hairs. As the "solute" (a useful cousin to the term "solution") moves into the root, a sort of border is reached. Called the Casparian strip, this border is a complete cylinder running parallel to the root's axis, and it acts as the plant's customs office. Needed ions are transported across the strip by chemical carrier molecules (bonded agents), and moved inward to appropriate cell membranes. Toxic, unwanted, or excess ions (undesirable aliens) are left at the surface of the root. Iron, for example, is an element that plants require very little of. Rushes and cattails growing in water with high iron content can reject so much of this element that they frequently develop tiny metallic crusts around their roots.

Indoor plant experts recommend periodic "flushing" of plant pots by putting on an excess of water and allowing it to drain out the bottom of the pot. The reason for this is based on the same mechanism of ion rejection. The normal complement of salts and ions added in tap water (and occasional fertilizer) will gradually build up around roots, since the plant uses large quantities of water but only a fraction of its ions. In the natural situation, the excess and rejected ions drain downward below the rooting zone, or are used by a neighboring plant. In a pot, they have nowhere to go. If the pot is never flushed, these rejected molecules eventually build up to very high concentrations and their osmotic grip on the water around them gets very tight. So tight, in fact, that the plant can no longer draw the water into itself. This "physiological drought," as it is called, is like dying of thirst on a salty ocean.

Similar processes occur in closed saline basins like Old Wives' Lake. Because of low rainfall, minimal stream recharge, high evaporation, and heavy soils, normal downward flushing of soil chemical elements is minimal. Glacial till frequently contains high background levels of calcium, potassium and magnesium salts. In closed basins, the salts migrate laterally with groundwater flow towards the lowest point in the basin. As the groundwater seeps upward, joining surface water and finally evaporating, its salts are left behind in the first few centimeters of soil.

Many chemical salts are useful. Farmers and gardeners work closely with the basic nutrients nitrogen, phosphorous, and potassium, but 13 other elements are known to be essential to plant growth. In addition to these, the plant root must be able to recognize and respond correctly to a host of other free enzymes, polysaccharides, virus particles, allelopaths, chelates, humic acids, and soil pollutants.

I have a perennial attraction to places like Old Wives, but that year I waited until September to visit, when the dust, drought, and political heat had settled. The outer margin of the lakebed was by then quite dry, and absolutely level. Landscape was reduced to blue sky, chocolate brown earth, and dusty white salt. The profound emptiness made even the smallest objects stand out: a small rock, a muskrat skull, or some old bulrush roots, evidence of a less saline past.

There was a small island in the middle of the lake, now just a height of land, called Pelican Island, inaccessible because of soft mud at the center of the lakebed, and continuously distorted by the mirage. It was easy to imagine it full of exotic vegetation, old bones, and pelican rookeries.

Old Wives' has been a curious and quirky lake. It has swallowed buffalo herds and World War II military aircraft. Some say the cackle of the old wives can be heard in the wind. A derelict sodium sulfate extracting plant molders on its southeast shore, the corrugated tin of its decrepit buildings flapping loosely in the ever present wind. The few farmsteads along the shoreline are mostly abandoned, recalling Palliser's dictum that the area was uninhabitable. Huge flocks of migratory waterfowl suddenly appear. Major flushes and collapses of new shoreline vegetation can come and go unnoticed.

One of those curious flushes was occurring in 1988, in the northwest corner. Kochia, an aggressive, salt-tolerant, weedy annual, was actively colonizing an area of near-shore lakebed.

Approaching this kochia zone from the lake side, a definite vegetative front was apparent: rising out of barren, windswept lakebed was a solid, 100-meter wide band of healthy, waist-high kochia. Moving into the kochia, one could see small piles of soil drift accumulated around stem bases, evidence that the dense and wiry growth was slowing the wind and allowing the airborne soil to settle out.

Moving further shoreward, the kochia became shorter and less vigorous. Isolated clumps of suaeda, a salt-tolerant perennial forb, began to appear. Moving further inward, one began to encounter the mat-forming desert saltgrass, and only occasional kochia plants. At the original shoreline itself, stable perennial saltgrass prairie vegetation prevailed.

The reason for kochia's disappearance at the shoreline is based on a phenomenon known as auto-allelopathy. Kochia and certain other "pioneer" plants sow the seeds of their eventual destruction by releasing a toxin into the soil that retards their own future growth. A new stand of kochia will grow unhindered in the first year, set seed, and die. Seeds germinating in a second-year stand have a tougher time of it. The toxin has accumulated to the point where plants are stunted and barely reach maturity. In the third year, the unidentified toxin reaches a level that simply wipes the species out. However, in these three years several significant things have occurred. Windspeed at ground level is reduced; soil-to-plant nutrient cycling begins; surface salt accumulation slows down; soil temperatures moderate; some snowfall is trapped and held. Other non-pioneer species, like suaeda or desert saltgrass, creep into the niche behind kochia.

No one has yet come up with an evolutionary logic for pioneer-plant allelopathy. It is tempting to make a case for a kind of vegetational Gaia, with kochia looking forward to the interests of suaeda, and suaeda to the desert saltgrass. Is auto-allelopathy a sacrifice of individual species for the good of the plant community, or just an intriguing accident? We simply don't know.

The proposed engineering solution to the Old Wives Lake problem was a classic mechanistic one that did no credit to the profession. Even if the large sums of money for drilling a well had been available, the water brought to the surface would have been loaded with minerals, further compounding the salt problem. Some of the world's largest potash (potassium chloride) mines are not far from Old Wives' Lake. The subterranean brine of ancient seas is not to be toyed with.

The fact that the lake went dry was not the problem, except for the long-suffering white pelican. The real problem was salty dust blowing off the dry lakebed. Kochia, if allowed (or even encouraged) to propagate in the temporary lakebed niche, could reduce or even eliminate the problem.

The little piles of windblown soil around the stem bases of those colonizing kochia plants seem insignificant next to the built technology of structural steel and reinforced concrete. But there is a certain elegance and forward harmony in the adaptations of pioneer plants like kochia. These mechanisms are the technologies of a niche-based ecological engineering, one that we would do well to study.

Bragg Creek, Alberta

Bragg Creek is a privileged part of Alberta, of the world for that matter. It lies in what ecologists call a zone of tension, where montane forest vegetation does pleasant battle with prairie. Fingers of each mesh together. The two armies of these Rocky Mountain wars have battled so long and honorably that they begin to look like each other: prairie is long and shaggy, and the open woods are full of grass.

This is also a kind of zone of human tension where the wealthy from nearby Calgary build monumental ranch homes, movie stars seek expensive refuge, and fourth-generation foothills cattlemen study the *I Ching*.

A group of us came to Bragg Creek for a week to discuss grazing ecology, and our classroom meetings were surprisingly long and intense. The woods and fields outside the classroom were inviting, but they began to look more distant and inaccessible as our seminar hurried on with few breaks.

Midmorning on the third day I was finally able to slip out. I needed to distance myself from the coffee-laden, fluorescent press of the seminar for a while. Skulking across the lawn, I headed for the safety of the white spruce. As I got close, my steps slowed and my attention began to shift from escape to observation. I knew I was safe now. Even if someone called me, I could simply pretend I didn't hear. As soon as I was safely into the woods, I felt silly for being so furtive.

Rising modestly into the still winter air, the bodies of the spruce were intimate and enfolding. I had the strong sense they had been waiting for me.

I followed the small creek. Neruda was right: perhaps the highest duty of the poet and writer is to waste time while others work. Awareness is sharpened, and the nagging sense of guilt eggs one on to ever more daring and secret explorations.

It is surprising how much is green here, even in early March: the spruce, the labrador tea underneath, the aquatic plants in the creek itself. This forest still has a tenuous hold on the previous summer. I can see why this was a favored wintering area for the buffalo.

I walk along the creek, trying to read its cutbanks. The colors and textures of the raw earth are unexpected, like nakedness. Revelations abound in these exposures of soil and rock and root. Layers of meaning are tucked in between sand lenses, organic stains, and bits of old bone. Here in front of me, if I could only read it, is a tiny sedimentary history of the Rockies.

I often stop to study cutbanks, gravel pits, and roadcuts. I dig deep holes in fields and puzzle over the complex horizons below me. But I haven't looked long enough, and can't yet read the language.

Veering away at random from the creek, I stop to sit on a spruce stump. It is freshly cut and honey-colored phloem sap still oozes from it. Off in the undergrowth, long strands of spider silk are shot through with random sunbeams. Wind riffles down the strands, and they become exotic neon. Ravens croak high overhead and the creek talks to itself like a contented child. The moment holds, as if cast in amber, and I think I know why. Patterns again, patterns and high-angle spring sun.

Some of our seminar discussions dealt with alternate realities, although few would have been prepared to admit to that. I am interested in alternate realities – not levitations, spoon bending and things like that, but the very personal ones that can flit unexpectedly through our lives. I don't see great pinwheels of fire in the sky like Blake and Van Gogh did, and I am probably not capable of the personal intensity behind that kind of alternate vision. But at just the right time of evening I can look at these shapely masses of spruce and see them neatly outlined in bright electric blue against the indigo of sky. Fiery winter sundogs can sometimes multiply across the sky for me. On bright winter days, black fenceposts against white snow can throw pale extensions of themselves into the air, in the style of the German impressionist painter Lyonel Feininger.

I don't know whether these are purely physical/optical phenomena, or whether the mind, and desire, are involved. I don't know if these experiences are unique to me. I guess I want them to be, since visions don't share well. But in any case, I am grateful for them. They are another kind of understanding, beyond data.

The seminar leader argues that a holistic view of reality cannot coexist with the contemporary scientific and reductionist view. Holism, he says, is a thought model that considers all variables at once, but the scientific model of testing a single variable at a time destroys the essence of real-world systems. I don't know. We humans tend naturally to be rather woolly thinkers, forever bringing things in from left field and cobbling them on to the issue at hand. A meeting on aid to El Salvador will turn into a heated discussion on war toys, or a committee looking into stocking rates will go off on an engrossing tangent of modifications to parliamentary procedure. And so on. It is our nature to be free-form, hot-dog, and eclectic; we live holism. So reductionist science, if nothing else, is probably a useful foil to lives full of concatenated events. A method to test things one at a time, as a check on ourselves.

The scientific method as a thought process has a splendid track record of progress. It is predictable then that an analytical tool this powerful would eventually be turned inward, on itself. The scientific method tries to establish a relationship between cause and effect, but several scientists have taken the method to hyperbole, and have begun to analyze our understanding of cause and effect themselves.

Subjects in an experiment are told to operate a simple electronic random number generator, to produce a normally distributed trend line of numbers. In a second trial, the subjects are asked to try to influence the generator as they operate it, to produce numbers either below or above the mean. After several thousand tries, sure enough, the trend line of the influenced trials begins to deviate from normal random expectations, and the deviations pass the test of statistical significance. The Princeton scientists who did this work call the effect "anomalous information transfer from an agent (the subject) to a percipient (the random number generator) who are separated geographically and not connected by any normal information channels." The subject's pushing of a button to activate a circuit is the obvious connection between cause and effect, but the scientists are telling us that there are other, less obvious connections as well.

This line of research is profoundly interesting. If corroborated and supported by other work, it could eventually lead to a wholesale rethinking of the scientific method as an objective tool.

Perhaps more important is the possibility of subtle information transfer from the perceived *back* to the perceiver, laying the foundation for our need for landscape. Rocks and grasses and mountains may have influence, something aboriginal cultures acknowledge and we have long suspected.

I came back to the lodge just in time for a noon meal and a volleyball game. The net was tied between two of several white spruce that some perceptive landscaper had left scattered about the large lawn. My context for volleyball had always been gymnasiums, and here was a pleasant contrast. As I went up for a spike, I looked up to see a white spruce like a sentinel, the ball descending perfectly to the net, and the brassy noonday sun. Often I mistime the spiking ritual, but this time I hammered the ball perfectly.

The seminar wore on relentlessly. After four days of theory, we finally broke away from our meeting room to actually visit nearby grassland to speculate on how grazing had affected it. An impressive collection of vans and pickups descended on a humble quarter-section, and some 50 of us jumped out. Many of the talismans of field biology began to appear: binoculars, bound floras, magnifying lenses, Swiss Army knives. The pasture was pleasant and shaggy, full of willow clumps and mole excavations. At some point there must have been abundant aspen growth on it, since many old sticks and stumps were visible. Now only two gnarled, dying specimens remained, their trunks rubbed smooth by cattle.

My comrade Barry Adams says that Peter Fidler rode through this country in 1792, and it was grassland then. Such a pure grassland, in fact, that Fidler complained in his journals about having to haul firewood along. So the recent evolution of this piece of ground would have been from grassland to aspen forest, and then back to the present hodgepodge cow-pasture grassland. These two trees must be the last diehards of the most recent rout of the army of the woods.

On casual inspection, I counted at least half a dozen grass species. Willow shrubs were everywhere in the pasture, and there was evidence that cattle were browsing on them. Shrubby cinquefoil was also here in abundance, but nothing was touching it. Silly and inappropriate plants like timothy and white clover were also present, two cultivated species that don't belong in native grassland. In this case cows must be acting as mechanisms of succession. They would have been moved to this pasture from some cultivated pasture somewhere, bringing seeds of the exotics in their rumens. The timothy and white clover seed would have come out in the manure, a moist, sheltered environment, and promptly added two new species to the general confusion.

When all our individual inspections were finished, we gathered near one of the crippled aspens. The pasture soon became a battleground of ideologies competing to explain its humble processes. Tense discussions were waged over soil compaction, stocking rate, selective grazing, nutrient recycling, and the herd effect. Bearded range managers fought with new wave ecologists, and wildlifers clashed with cattlemen. No quarter was given. Fescue, pussytoes, and grasshopper eggs were trampled in the heat of discussion. The seminar leader had a comprehensive explanation for everything, which was rejected as too simplistic, but then none of the competing explanations were strong enough to carry the day. At length we finally gave up and returned to our vehicles. Everyone was dissatisfied.

We left the rusty brown cinquefoil in silence, and returned to blackboards and flow charts, eventually to disperse. The motley collection of pasture flora got back to waiting for another turn at spring and the ongoing mystery of grazing.

I think about that shaggy pasture often, and wonder what might have helped us to truly understand it. We created our own kind of tension there, but mostly in the negative zone of professional ego. We based our theories on conventional (and hyperconventional) observation, and failed to reach any true understanding of the Bragg Creek landscape. Perhaps others trained in different modes of observation – poets, or painters – could have aided us, drawn out patterns or connections or contexts that we couldn't see. Or perhaps each of us should have stolen out to that pasture, individually and furtively, to explore fleeting visions of it that might not quite match reality.

The Soil-Plant-Atmosphere Continuum

Plants are spouts, through which a significant part of the earth's water is drawn back into the atmosphere. Grassy dells, green mansions, and verdant bowers all suck voraciously at the ground beneath them, and spray their water as fine vapor back into the sky. A major loop in the global water cycle passes through plants, and this liquid continuum shapes their destiny, perhaps more than anything else. The amount and timing of water determines where aspen parkland grades into mixed prairie, where stipa grass gives way to blue grama, and where lodgepole pine takes over from bluebunch wheatgrass. Rain will bring soil crust algae to life for a precious few hours. Winter precipitation is equally important: the depth of winter snow cover is a primary determinant in the distribution of many plant species in the northern prairies.

Without delving into the complexities of water deficit measurement, one can visualize how plants relate to water by visualizing the sky as a great magnet for water. The sheer size of the atmosphere and its dryness relative to the earth do make it a powerful sink for water, except for those periods when water is given back as precipitation. Moisture from the earth leaps into the sky, following the immutable physical law that forces gases – like water vapor – to constantly attempt to equalize their concentration in space. If the ground is bare, soil water will evaporate directly into the air. If plants cover the soil surface, then most soil water is transpired through plants, and departs from earth by way of tiny stomata on leaf surfaces.

Plants have harnessed this upward movement of water so adroitly that it is tempting to think they themselves pump water from their roots up to distant leaves. They do not. Water in the plant xylem is responding to a physical, atmospheric drive – evaporation – that is much stronger than any force a plant could produce on its own. The difference in the vapor pressure inside a leaf and that of the air one millimeter above the leaf can be three orders of magnitude. That difference is the engine of water movement in all higher plants – in every species from pygmy flower to a 95-meter sitka spruce.

We have already seen how water is pulled into the plant root and shorn of its ions by the Casparian strip. This purified water is then propelled upward, forming an unbroken column from the root hairs, clear through the intricacies of stem and branch xylem, and finally to the leaf mesophyll cells. The whole column is drawn slowly upward, responding to the powerful suction forces created by evaporation at the leaf surface. Under normal, non-stress conditions, a milliliter of water pulled through the stomata into the atmosphere means that another milliliter of water is pulled from the soil into the roots.

Final control over plant water is vested in the thousands of stomata – microscopic, adjustable valves – on the leaf surface.

Underneath these stomata is a dense layer of chlorophyll-bearing cells that trap sunlight and do most of the photosynthesis. Underneath this palisade layer is a spongy and porous layer called the mesophyll. The cells of the mesophyll are the actual sites of evaporation.

On the prairies, midsummer conditions are usually so extreme that most plants open their stomata only at night and early morning. The wind and sun of midday create such tremendous transpiration (leaf water evaporation) rates that soil water recharge cannot keep up. The stomata close in response to this stress.

Plants differ in their ability to handle water stress. Tender, leafy plants like the tomato have poor control over water loss, with large, porous leaf areas and many stomata. The unfortunate tomato is helpless in situations of water stress, and responds by emptying its xylem and tissue cells of water. The result is catastrophic wilting. Tissues normally held rigid by water-swollen cells will collapse, leaving nothing more than a pathetic green ribbon on the ground.

Near the other end of the scale are the native wheatgrasses, stipas and gramas of our dry grasslands. Leaves of these plants contain lots of dry, almost woody supporting tissue along with the normal leaf tissues. They can withstand extreme water loss and simply go dormant rather than wilt. Cells of these grasses contain quantities of dissolved carbohydrates and proteins that act as an osmotic "sink" to draw in more water.

In between the drought tolerant and non-tolerant species are the so-called "drought avoiders" that count on speed and spring moisture to complete their life cycle. One of my favorites in this genre is a spring ephemeral called trailing vetch. This tiny legume can be quite thick on early spring prairie if moisture is good. It is a vine, sprouting vigorously from a large seed and using its curling tendrils to ride to sunlight and space on the backs of neighboring grasses.

The vining habit of trailing vetch is a clever tactic. By eliminating the need for rigid structural tissue, it can concentrate its energies on rapid leaf, flower and seed production, cutting weeks off its life cycle and avoiding the dry months of July and August.

Junegrass, another drought avoider, is a major constituent of mixed and shortgrass prairie in springs of average or above average moisture. In dry springs junegrass and trailing vetch simply vanish, as if they were never a part of the flora. But they are there, patiently waiting.

Range ecologists are occasionally stunned by sudden explosions of new plants, especially broadleaved annuals, that have not been seen on a particular site for years. The visible, growing flora is only part of the vast plant catalogue suspended in the soil. Seeds of these sequestered plants await their particular combination of time, sun, water, and disturbance that will allow them to form part of the fragile buffer between earth and sky.

On the Outlier

I drive slowly as we make the ascent from Maple Creek, curious to see the effect as prairie is heaved into the air. But the climb is very gradual, and nothing much happens. The folded hills yield aspen clumps and, here and there, a dirty spring snowbank. We continue to climb, more steeply now, and at 1250 meters a remarkable change occurs: the hills have leveled out to a flat, unglaciated plateau covered with a secret forest of lodgepole pine.

Even as we unpack, this forest beckons. Little grows under the dense lodgepole, and the ground is a springy bed of needles. Prairie-weary, I am drawn into this dim, grayish-green aquarium of repetitive, branchless trunks.

The climax vegetation of the Cypress Plateau would likely be a mosaic of lodgepole pine and fire-maintained rough fescue grassland. Because of the modern absence of fire, the Plateau has gone to a lodgepole disclimax. Like other communities dominated by a single species, this one seems to teeter on the brink of disaster. Forest officials live in fear of bark beetle invasions and catastrophic fires. Tree blowdowns and snow damage are commonplace. The crowded pines compete fiercely for sunlight and growing space. They throw all their resources into upward growth, so root systems are minimal, stems are fragile, and lower branches non-existent.

As I begin to adjust to this new environment, I notice a subtle atmosphere of pine resin, altitude, and euphoria. Thirty meters up, a strong spring breeze bends and ruffles the branches of these sunlight warriors. Down here on the forest floor there is complete calm.

The children are busy exploring around the cabin, my wife is taking a catnap, and the folks are planning supper. I slip a bit further out in the woods, and my stride lengthens. Walking on this forest floor is so easy that two or three kilometers come quickly, almost as an afterthought. I notice a few poplars and willows are able to creep into the draws, but on level ground the lodgepole stand is absolutely pure. Stopping, I feel small muscle pains deep in my upper thighs. I have not been aware of these recondite muscles in my usual life of city streets and bureaucratic stairways, so they must be mountain muscles, open-country muscles. I begin feeling like the tentative king of the woods. Jeremiah Johnson in Converse low-cuts.

Returning, I concentrate and lay out my course in a straight line, guided by intuition and the compass that floats in the brain. Miss the cabin by 300 meters. Dead reckoning sense intact, but rusty.

The next morning I am vegetating on the cabin porch when my dad presents me with an old fly rod he brought with him. I have always felt something special about fly fishing, that it is one of the more elegant adaptations of man to his environment.

I learned the craft in the Okanagan and had nearly forgotten it since moving to the prairies, where trout are a rarity. But there is a small lake here on the outlier, and I hurry down to try it.

The rod is a lovely instrument, a "Governor" model, made of split cane from the Gulf of Tonkin. It works beautifully. The Governor and I go on to spend a good part of the next few days working the lake, the streams and the beaver ponds of Cypress. The results are disappointing. One old fellow passing by tells me the trout haven't been stocked yet this year, and any carryover is usually claimed by the blue herons in the spring. Trout are mountain fish, and I guess they aren't very comfortable here on the outlier.

The one chance the Governor and I have to perform is with a feisty perch. All the Okanagan moves come back automatically. The first move — setting the hook — is the confirmation of several hypotheses rather than mere gut reaction. Then the arms go up, the elbows go out, like a conductor. Slack line in the right hand, pole in left. This pole tapers to a mere twig and the leader to a hair, so every move is communicated between us. The Governor and I do not fight this perch to shore, rather we offer him a compelling invitation.

The last evening before we are to leave, I propose one last try for trout. So we all troop off to a set of beaver ponds I haven't fished yet, a string of deep and quiet pearls. They are almost too good. The water is still, there is a hatch of lacewings, and the kids are busy with their spinning rods. The folks sit on the bank, savoring small pieces of grandparenthood. I perceive everything to be right about these ponds, but incredibly, there are no fish. My perceptions are dead wrong. Gut-level limnology has failed me completely, because this water contains some hidden trout-flaw.

I continue to make futile casts into perfect water as nightfall gathers vaguely in the willows along the far bank. Looking up, I realize the beavers are about. They probably waited patiently for us to leave, but there was work to be done and they had to get on with it. Beavers always seemed small to me, but these two come right up close and I see they are massive, powerful animals, confident of their work and their survival. They come at us repeatedly, slapping and diving at the last minute. We watch until complete darkness and finally leave, with regrets.

My Canadian identity is somehow tangled up with these beavers, and I am pleased to see their confidence. Trout exist here only at the pleasure of game biologists and government budgets, but beaver are part of this outlier. They fit neatly into all the things the trout don't mesh with: the spring runoff levels, siltation rates, dissolved oxygen levels, and the lodgepole.

There are moments during this stay when I have been content to simply observe, breathe in the various essences of this place, and be a part of it. But at other times, I am conscious of a great empty hole in these woods. That hole is the absence of things to do. None of the comfortable diversions are found here: no confectionery errands, no lawn, no newspapers. So all of us tend to fill that void with various pursuits of movement, going through the woods on skis, snowmobiles or groaning campers. Or we busy ourselves by capturing things, like game, rocks, or even flowers. Simple stasis is hard to achieve.

I have tried to eliminate some of these confounding activities of movement and capture over the years, to better deal with the woods on their own terms. The biggest break came when I sold a venerable old shotgun I received as a boy of 12. The Browning got me out in the woods a great deal, hunting ducks and pheasant with my father. Later on I would simply carry it in the crook of my arm, in the company of a useless but friendly beagle. The sale of the gun was a painful but healthy parting. Over the years I had come to see it as a prop, and no longer essential to the satisfaction I derived from my outings. This family is now unarmed, probably for the first time since the dawn of gunpowder.

Fly fishing still stays with me though. Either as a throwback, or an activity close to stasis, I am not sure which.

Perhaps there are other positive activities for these woods. Since we feel compelled to come here with some purpose, I have designed something called the Species Evolution Activity. It is really an anti-program, though, since nothing much happens when you do it.

To start, the individual first gathers some physiological knowledge about the species populating the woods. Then, after some preparatory walking, he or she finds a comfortable spot, and sits down. The thick carpet of needles is pleasant, and the lodgepole backrest transmits subtle impulses from the wind and sky above the canopy. The person allows the environment to flow inward, and soon accumulated knowledge fuses with sense. All that remains now are fully-tuned eyes, ears, nose and skin. Slowly, questions arrive, like small brown birds.

– What brings that squirrel headfirst down the tree?
– How long does it take for the fallen lodgepole to rot if it snags above the ground?
– What mechanisms allow the odd shrub and grass to survive on this dim and needle-choked forest floor?
– What physiological strings are being plucked right now, at this precise solar moment?

Just as naturally as these questions arise, they are rendered transparent and obvious by the fully tuned and molecular senses.

Prizes for this exercise seem out of place, but if necessary they could be awarded to the person who achieves Inner Tranquillity (third prize) or a Sense of Place (second prize). First prize would go to the entrant who actually Feels Evolution Occurring, who senses some minute increase in the appropriateness of species response.

If I practice this, the Outlier may yield some of its secrets. Instead of coming away with captured things, I may some day come away with the private biological gossip of the beaver, the lodgepole, and the absent trout.

Hugh Kortschack, Pineapples and the C4 Syndrome

The relationship between plant breeders and industry has always been very close. Agronomists and weed control specialists also get on well with their corporate bosses. Plant physiologists, on the other hand, are somewhat suspect, being like particle physicists or dead language experts. Employers rarely understand what these people do, and often assume their work is essentially frivolous.

I once knew a physiologist who was making great progress in developing a theory of plant growth responses while working at a weed research station. But he lived with an edge of fear, because the station's main activity was herbicide testing. He was convinced that one day his director would come into the lab and say, "Arthur, either kill some weeds or get out."

One of the great discoveries in modern plant physiology occurred under similar circumstances. Hugh Kortschack worked as a physiologist at a small research station in Hawaii that was funded by the Sugar Planters' Association. Increased sugarcane production was the goal of the station's research, and Kortschack and his colleagues were looking at the photosynthetic efficiency of this plant. In the late 1950s, while conducting some experiments using radioactively labeled carbon dioxide, they found some erratic and interesting results.

By allowing their sugarcane test plants to take up the labeled carbon dioxide and then flash-freezing leaf samples in a time series after uptake, they found they could follow the chemical transformations of the labeled carbon dioxide on its way toward becoming sugar. The general pathways of this process had been recently worked out, and Kortschack looked forward to seeing labeled carbon turning up in the expected three-carbon acids, the precursors of sugar. To everyone's surprise, most of the label turned up as four-carbon acids.

This kind of information was not of much use to the Hawaiian Sugar Planters' Association. In fact, it was probably the kind of esoteric finding that produces employer paranoia, so Kortschack didn't take the work much farther. But he knew he had something. Eventually he persuaded two Australian research physiologists, Hatch and Slack, to pursue the four-carbon anomaly.

Hatch and Slack picked up the ball admirably. Five years later, with their long-suffering employer, the Commonwealth Scientific and Industrial Research Organization (CSIRO), proudly looking on, they presented the world with three separate, mutually exclusive pathways for the uptake of carbon in higher plants. All three types share the common bond of photosynthesis, and all use carbon dioxide, water and solar energy to produce short-chain carbon compounds. Depending on their need and inclination, all three will go on to build these short-chain acids into carbohydrates, like sugars, starches, or lignin (wood). Within this common framework though, Hatch and Slack found major differences: separate pathways for producing the initial short-chain compounds, different key enzymes, different leaf microanatomy, and different plant adaptations. The first of the variants is called C3-type metabolism, and it is characteristic of most native and cultivated plants of the temperate zone, with a few notable exceptions. In C3 plants, carbon fixation (the chemical entrapment of carbon dioxide in the leaf) is driven by an enzyme that goes by the unlovely name of ribulose biphosphate carboxylase, RuBp carboxylase for short. (A key enzyme for life as we know it should have a more elegant name.) RuBp carboxylase performs the simple and incredibly vital task of linking a new carbon from carbon dioxide to existing carbon-chain molecules in the plant. The three-carbon acids produced are the raw materials for maple sugar, two-by-fours, digitalis, and ten thousand other wonderful things.

Plants of the second type, the C4, have a different carbon fixing enzyme called PeP carboxylase. This enzyme also takes a carbon from carbon dioxide, but it produces four-carbon instead of three-carbon acids.

The fact that enzymes RuBp and PeP carboxylase produce different first products is trivial. The big difference between these enzymes is their efficiency. Enzymes have a property of affinity, a measure of how much they like their raw materials. To measure this, one invokes equations devised by mathematicians with sonorous names like Arrhenius and Michaelis-Menten. Suffice it to say that when the C3 and C4 enzyme affinities are compared, the C4 enzyme excels; it is very hungry for carbon dioxide, and can scour it from the atmosphere even at very low concentrations. In fact, one of the diagnostic tests for C4 metabolism is to put the test plant in a closed chamber and allow the carbon dioxide to slowly deplete. If the plant continues to function when carbon dioxide levels are extremely low, then that is conclusive evidence for the presence of PeP carboxylase and thus C4 metabolism.

In addition to being a hungrier enzyme, the C4 enzyme has a higher ideal temperature range — around 25 to 30 degrees — than the C3 enzyme, which peaks somewhere between 20 and 25 degrees centigrade.

Differences occur in leaf anatomy as well. In C3 plants, the productive mesophyll cells are in a honeycomb layer sandwiched between the palisade cells on the top and bottom of the leaf. Finished carbon products move out of these mesophyll cells to regularly spaced phloem tubes. Those cells close to a phloem tube export their products quickly, but for the more distant cells, movement is slow and laborious, like the commuter trying to get through spaghetti suburbs to the expressway.

Leaves of C4 plants are arranged very differently. The mesophyll cells are not dispersed in a layer, but are wrapped in concentric rings around the phloem tubes. Gottfried Haberlandt, the canny German botanist who uncovered large sections of the C4 tapestry in the 1880s, called this cell arrangement "kranz" (German for "wreath") anatomy. The name has stuck.

The C4 anatomical differences are not frivolous. When the products of a chemical reaction stay in place and build up, the reaction that produces them slows down and eventually stops, due to a phenomenon called "feedback inhibition." Haberlandt saw that the C3 architecture, forcing the product to move through many mesophyll cells until reaching a phloem export tube, encouraged feedback inhibition (he called it "denial of immediate egress"). The C4 architecture appeared much more efficient, with the productive mesophyll cells grouped tightly around phloem tubes in such a way that new photosynthate products could be moved out quickly.

The third metabolic variant is called Crassulacean Acid Metabolism (CAM), and is typical of the fleshy-leaved desert plants, like cactus (*Crassulacea* sp., the ornamental jade, is the benchmark plant of this group). CAM plants use the same metabolic scheme as the C4 plants, but their art comes in the scheduling of metabolic events. All plants can stagger photosynthesis and carbon uptake to some extent, but the CAM plants, because of the brutal environments they are adapted to, separate the events completely. Daytime for a CAM plant is given over strictly to photosynthesis and the production of the three-carbon acceptor molecules. The stomata stay tightly shut all day. No carbon dioxide gets in, but no water escapes, either. When the heat and water stress starts to decrease at sundown, stomata open and all the three-carbon chains produced during the day are put to work accepting carbon dioxide. CAM plants grow very slowly as a result, but they can survive for months without water.

The buildup of acid, 3-carbon storage compounds makes CAM plants taste bitter during the day. At night they gradually become sweet again as carbons are added through fixation and sugars are produced. That is why pineapples are harvested in the early morning hours.

CAM plants have standard kranz anatomy, but the gross morphology of these plants is always distinct: they are thick-leaved and fleshy, like cacti, the jade plant, and pineapple. This is an adaptation to stress environments; thickening increases volume without greatly increasing exposed surface area.

As the biochemical pieces are gradually fitted into this ecophysiological puzzle, an incredible pattern begins to emerge. The pattern can be seen clearly in the table of representative C3, C4 and CAM species. The C4 group has a kind of tropical lineage to it, and includes some of the noble grasses like sugarcane and bamboo. The C4 plants simply grow faster than C3's. Since they fix carbon dioxide quickly, growth can continue even though stomata are partially closed to reduce water loss. It is not surprising then that we find some really successful agricultural crops in this group, like corn and sorghum, and some devastating weeds as well, like green foxtail, pigweed, kochia, Russian thistle, and portulaca.

REPRESENTATIVE SPECIES OF THE THREE METABOLIC KINGDOMS

C3	C4	CAM
apple	corn	pincushion cactus
rose	sugarcane	prickly pear cactus
wheat	bamboo	pineapple
barley	portulaca	agave
tomato	russian thistle	jade plant
wheatgrass	green foxtail	salicornia
alfalfa	blue grama	
bean	big bluestem	
all conifers	barnyard grass	
marigold	goosegrass	
junegrass	pigweed	
needlegrass	kochia	

Few plants in the CAM group find uses in agriculture, probably because they grow so slowly. Pineapple is a significant exception, and then there is agave, the spiny "century plant," which gives us baling twine and tequila.

There is speculation that C4 plants developed at a time when the earth's atmosphere had little carbon dioxide in it, and they stayed on to this day because their metabolic efficiency gives them an edge. Since we as a species seem bent on putting even more carbon dioxide into the atmosphere, and warming it as well, we will be favoring the C4 plants, up to a point. This fact is frequently touted by the apologists for the industrial corruption of our atmosphere.

There is another possible C4 adaptation that I am curious about. During my days in the greenhouse, I noticed that the C4 grasses had several leaves developing simultaneously on each tiller, whereas the C3 grasses developed only one leaf at a time, sequentially. Since new photosynthetic tissue is very efficient, a grass that can produce a lot of it quickly may have an advantage.

The prairie environment is far distant from a tropical one, yet there are a surprising number of C4 plants here. Blue grama grass, the short, curly, mat-former found on uplands, is the prototype, the prairie benchmark C4. It can be found as far north as Prince Albert. Big bluestem, a component of the true Tallgrass Prairie, is a C4 native to southeastern Saskatchewan and southwestern Manitoba, but its lush habitat has been all but lost to the breaking plow. Little bluestem is found on very specific, subirrigated hillside niches throughout the prairies and the southern British Columbia interior.

The C4's of the Canadian prairies tend to be in the extreme environments of sand dune, saline flat, cultivated field or dry hillside. Supercharged metabolism has given this group of plants a bold approach to life. Vernon Harms, a botanist from the University of Saskatchewan, found an assumed C4 called tangled panic grass nestled in the sand dunes near Cluff Lake, Saskatchewan. Hitchcock's *Manual of the Grasses* describes tangled panic as a species native to the moist, sandy woodlands of Georgia. So this Cluff Lake individual was roughly 3000 kilometers north of its home range. Nobody knows how it got there.

The work of Hugh Kortschack opened a Pandora's box that great numbers of plant investigators are still rummaging around in. The biochemical work is fairly well done, but now we face the much more ambiguous and frustrating studies of the meaning of these pathways in a field situation. Biochemical hypotheses can be tested in a laboratory, with proof or disproof in the form of reaction maps, scintillation counts and so on. But testing a hypothesis on the function of that piece of biochemistry in nature yields ambiguous proofs, cluttered with all the statistical trappings of faintly perceived trends. This is the kind of work plant ecologists do. If anything, they are probably more suspect than plant physiologists.

Perhaps the suspicion is healthy. Possessors of esoteric knowledge often have ivory tower attitudes, and the tension set up by working in an industrial environment like Kortschack did is probably creative. And I am willing to bet that at the annual meetings of the Hawaiian Sugar Planter's Association, in between the mai-tais and the financial statements, there is room for some grudging pride about the physiological revolution that their own Hugh Kortschack triggered so long ago.

Analogues and Desire

Exploration. *Explore* is a resonant word, a power center of our language. Those who gave the word its contemporary meaning entered new landscapes to record birdcalls, vegetation, and compass bearings, with passionate absorption. These explorers had omnivorous scientific interests, and they were monkish in their indifference to delays and discomfort. Their names, like those of Alexander von Humboldt, Samuel Hearne, John Wesley Powell, Lewis and Clark, John Palliser, and Henry Hind, read like a pantheon to me. Yet the real heroes may be those nameless men and women who first stepped onto the New World.

The Irishman John Palliser explored this region of mine, the Canadian West, to determine its suitability for permanent settlement, according to the mores of the Victorian era. His Report to Her Majesty of 1860 contains detailed descriptions of landforms in the four western provinces, as well as observations on vegetation and climate. Captain Palliser was particularly attracted to heights of land. It is an interesting exercise to read of his reactions to a particular butte or range of hills and compare them to one's own, 130 years later.

The modern day Triangle, that great swath of land named after Palliser, is now densely woven with underground gas pipelines, feedlots, and golf courses. Many of the dramatic heights of land he described are now staked with microwave transmission towers. Yet the Triangle is still hinterland, by any cosmopolitan North American standards. Could it not be further explored, or re-explored? What silent passing of attitude, or veneer of settlement, has stopped this pursuit, stopped us from calling ourselves explorers? What happened to noble and disinterested quests for knowledge of our earth?

Palliser, together with his geologist Hector and the botanist Bourgeau, explored the prairies with only compass, theodolite and notebooks. They had no access to computerized weather modeling, no false-color infrared satellite imagery, no neutron-activated soil moisture probes, no historical databases. Should we ever care to explore again, as opposed to simply researching, the tools we have available are stunning in their reach and sensitivity. All that is needed is the desire

There is a narrow plateau that winds east and west through the Palliser Triangle, a spine that starts as the Milk River Ridge in south central Alberta. Where it crosses into Saskatchewan, the formation is called the Cypress Hills, and farther to the east, as it winds down towards eastern Montana, it becomes Old Man on His Back, Pinto Horse Butte, Sevenmile, Twentymile, The Gap, Wood Mountain, the Killdeer Badlands, and so on. The plateau is a capricious landform. Only after walking the individual parts does it become obvious that they are indeed a geologic whole.

I am drawn to this plateau, in all its manifestations across the prairie. For years I have found reasons to go there, visiting ranchers, looking at pastures, or camping. Although it does contain the highest point on the prairies, most of the landform rises only a few hundred feet above prairie level. The north side, the side that faced the oncoming waves of Pleistocene glacier advance, slopes gradually, but the southern flanks are quite steep. Common characteristics all along the plateau are the rough, broken surface topography and the presence of rounded, flattened stones.

These stones have a long history. During the Cenozoic, great rivers of rock washed eastward out of the emerging Rocky Mountains as they buckled and rose above the plain. The abrasion of water and gravity rounded the edges of these stones and produced the characteristic cobblestones that range in size from a small potato to a dinner plate. Most of this accumulation of stone was later ground to silt by the Pleistocene glaciers, but the Cypress spine endured. It became an archipelago of reefs and islands barely rising above the glacier. The spine bought from the glacier an integrity and permanent wildness, paying the price with rough, unleveled topography and a thin soil full of cobblestones.

Finding deposits of these same granite cobblestones on parts of the spine that are seven or eight hundred kilometers apart gives a sense of the magnitude of Western Canadian geological events.

Captain Palliser mapped the boundaries of his famous Triangle, but made only one brief foray inside it. He was consistent with other explorers who were far more interested in the northern parts of Saskatchewan and Alberta than they were in the south. As a consequence the region of the Cypress spine is blank on these early maps. An RCMP map of 1875 gives a bit more detail, but it was not until the 1920s that cartographers recognized the Cypress landform and added it to their maps. Even today's maps define the plateau mainly by a discontinuity of roads and an absence of towns.

Looking closely at a modern hydrological map of the Cypress Hills area, I noticed two creeks that rose quite close to each other but flowed in opposite directions. Intrigued, I followed them on the map and discovered that a continental divide could be traced along part of the plateau. Creeks on one side of the divide trickled northward to the Saskatchewan, and those on the other fed into the Mississippi drainage.

Certain tracts of land focus elements of the landscape, physically and symbolically. The Cypress plateau does that; it is the geographical clasp, joining the Gulf of Mexico to the Arctic Ocean, and the Rockies to the prairies. This plateau saw the last of the free-ranging buffalo, and the last of the non-reservation Indian bands. And it is the only prairie landform not overridden by glaciers. In short, the plateau is an excellent candidate for reexploration.

Captain Palliser did his exploring on horseback. Lewis and Clark and John Wesley Powell moved largely by canoe, and von Humboldt explored South America on foot. Subtle differences of perspective originated from each mode of conveyance. Palliser measured the grasslands in terms of how well they could feed and water his horses. He would report the grass in one area as barely covering their hooves, but in another region it would graze their bellies.

I decided to end the casual trips to the plateau and start a systematic reexploration of it. My conveyance would be the bicycle.

A bicycle is everything the car is not: slow, quiet, open, with its capability measured mostly in human terms. A bicycle is directly connected to the land by wind, slope, and surface roughness. On a bike I would never be subject to those blank moments in automobiles when the landscape fades and consciousness shifts to neutral. I began to read all I could on bike touring and discovered it was a technology in full explosion. Frame geometry was new. Chromium and molybdenum alloys made the steel lighter and stronger. Luggage racks and panniers received lavish design and refinement. Tiny onboard bicycle computers could measure every time/velocity parameter you needed to know, plus several more that you didn't. In the end, I retrofitted an older, reliable 12-speed with racks, wider handlebars, and wider tires. There was a kind of packhorse reliability about the bike that seemed appropriate.

The first dawn of my bicycle re-exploration began at Battle Creek, near the Saskatchewan-Alberta border. I tried not to think about the threatening weather as I ground up the steep hill out of the valley. As the day broke I saw the sky was packed solid with thick gray cloud. The rain started soon after.

Okay. I had brought a cheap rain parka with me, and stopped to put it on. The topographical map I had strapped on the handlebar bag was getting wet, so that had to be stowed. I was counting on following its sinuous isolines as I rode along, but no matter.

The rain came steadily, slowly increasing in volume. Soon it became hard to ignore. This part of the bench was quite high, and the cloud layer seemed to start just above my head. The specially-purchased touring tires bit deeply into the softening gravel road. Mud mixed with coarse gravel began to gather between the wheel rims and chainstays, and I found I was pedaling harder and harder just to maintain a steady pace. At kilometer three of 40, I stopped.

Turning back was a bitter disappointment. My family had been skeptical about the trip, and the logistics of getting me and the bicycle to the starting point had not been easy. So much for conveyance, so much for exploration and endurance. I had been stopped by an ordinary summer rainshower.

Back at home I plunged into reading again, about glacial geology and head tube angles. Reexploration of the plateau by bicycle had started as a casual idea, but this first failed attempt helped to make it more significant to me. I had time to shape the trip in my mind, to color the grasses and fill in the clumps of lodgepole. The distances, the feeling of the road and the reasons were somewhat harder to visualize. But then we live our lives partly through these kinds of analogues and desire.

Two years later, I got another chance, on a glorious spring morning. The wretched kilometer three was behind me after only a few minutes, and I literally sailed up into the airborne and verdant hills. Black Angus cattle grazed on distant green slopes, against a backdrop of cumulus cloud and blue sky. Deep green of lodgepole on north faces. Those smooth and rounded stones, the size of dinner plates, that the children would take home to paint faces on. Rust-brown shrubby cinquefoil (the locals, not keen on French, call it "conkwell") growing thick in the draws. Demure and enduring prairie. Explorer, naturalist: these are the only true occupations.

From Battle Creek to Loch Lomond, a small lake within the Park boundary, was the first leg. The next day I struck out for Eastend, 50 kilometers away. The route took me off the top of the bench and down along its south flank. The bike was less of a worry now that I had a day of experience, although it hammered badly whenever I crossed the cobblestone outcrops, the silt of that great prehistoric river. At one point my front tire went flat on a long hill. I had never fixed a bicycle flat on the road before, but I simply replaced the tube with a new one I had brought along. Not as elegant as patching certainly, but it increased my confidence.

I stopped frequently to look at things, or just to look. At one stop I found a lovely marine fossil, *Receptaculites*, the same one found in Manitoba's famous Tyndal stone. This fossil has given paleontologists fits: first they called the round, symmetrical structure a sponge, but lately they have convinced themselves it was a great gob of algae. This one was embedded in a boulder the size of a suitcase. If I had come by car, I might have been tempted to load it up.

The white spruce and lodgepole dropped out as I came off the plateau. Now I was in plains rough fescue country, with admixtures of silver lupine, cinquefoil, and prairie sage. Rough fescue grass is the classic prairie wool; its long, narrow leaves are renowned for their ability to carry livestock through fall and winter. Rough fescue's range is (or was) that great crescent of land along the edge of the forest – the side and hypotenuse of Palliser's Triangle – plus the wetter zones of British Columbia's southern interior valleys, and the Cypress spine. Occasionally straight lines of stones stretched across the prairie, marking where an early settler had cleared them in order to cut the prairie wool for hay. The dream beds of the homesteader.

There was much to experience, not the least of which was the simple passage of rough grid road underneath my front wheel. I was totally alone on the landscape. Stopping once, I was about to lean the bike against a fencepost when I heard a sudden rushing noise nearby and saw a great commotion in the grass.

There was an aggressive, noisy catspaw, no more than two meters across, zigzagging through the grass in the midst of a calm, windless day. I watched the brief firework performance as a surprised and grateful spectator. I had seen the wind.

One of my plans for this exploration had been to start adding backpack technology — a small laptop, an altimeter, thermocouple soil temperature probes and so on, to complement a camera and binoculars. Part of the explorer's job is to produce data. But the attention those instruments would demand might have caused me to miss the catspaw.

At Ravenscrag my road joined the Frenchman River and followed it through a narrow bedrock valley. This landscape was the opposite of the plateau: a glacial meltwater channel that had cut deeply into the prairie. On the eroded slopes time lay exposed, right down to Cretaceous shales and Jurassic coal seams. Several bones from a Triceratops were found not far from here. This was indeed a privileged view. I felt a small measure of the awe of Powell in the Grand Canyon or Leakey in the African Rift; these valleys are the intimate labia of the earth itself.

The surrounding land gradually came back down to prairie level again, in a gap where the glacier had broken through the Cypress spine. Coming into Eastend, I detoured down a quiet residential side street to pass by the writer Wallace Stegner's old house. Stegner could perhaps assume the mantle of explorer on the strength of *Wolf Willow*. His work is rooted in land, in this charmed western space, and few things escaped his notice.

My family was waiting for me at the Greek cafe on main street, our rendezvous point. The kids were busy with french fries and hamburgers, and my youngest shared some of hers with me. I was tired and deeply satisfied.

We had to leave for home in the morning so the next leg, to Shaunavon and on to Val Marie, would be a while yet, and Wood Mountain was well beyond that. The Milk River Ridge country might be years away, and the mother Rockies sometime after that. But each new leg of the trip would grow and shape and root in my mind, like this one had. I know now that a private yearning and desire are essential to an age of exploration.

Watching the Grass Grow

At a certain microscopic scale, a leaf begins to lose its biological elegance and starts looking more like a clanking, humming factory. The factory image, in fact, is not far off the mark: a grass leaf is essentially a four-story, double-sided, solar-driven manufacturing plant, suspended in space. The roof of this factory is made from thick, transparent cuticle cells. Just below the roof, on the fourth floor, is a palisade layer, where photosynthesis takes place. The third floor is the spongy mesophyll layer we already know as the place where transpiration occurs. The second and first floors form the underside of the leaf, and they are a rough mirror image of the third and fourth. The stomata on the upper and lower roof vent gases and vapors to and from the mesophyll layer to the outside. Xylem and phloem liquid supply lines come in through the utility space between the second and third floors.

The interior leaf mesophyll cells are not just the site of water evaporation, they are also the locus for the absorption or "fixation" of carbon dioxide. Plants snatch carbon dioxide from the air around them and transform it into everything from duckweed to hemlock.

Here in the mesophyll lies the often desperate exchange that green plants must make: for every bit of carbon dioxide they allow in through their stomata, they lose a dribble of precious water (as vapor) via the same route. The prevention of water loss comes at the expense of carbon gain, and the access to carbon is paid for by lost water. A classic dilemma.

I was ignorant of the importance of this plant reality when I first started work in the research greenhouse. One of my first experiments was to attach a delicately-balanced recording boom to an emerging grass leaf. The other end of the boom was attached to a tiny pen which recorded movement on a slowly rotating drum. Upward growth of the leaf allowed the boom to rise, and the pen at the other end would dutifully record that movement on graph paper wrapped around the drum. "Length" is very nearly synonymous with "growth" in grass, making it a good choice for this experiment. My hypothesis was that leaf growth would start slowly just after sunrise, increase steadily until afternoon, and taper off to a halt at sundown.

When I pulled off the first inked charts I was innocently surprised. These plants grew all night! That violated all my childhood notions about photosynthesis. I redid the experiment with an even lighter boom, thinking that my apparatus was stretching the plants at night, like some medieval torture rack. Then I tried a different grass species, thinking that my first choice had been some sort of anomaly.

All the results were basically the same. Peak growth usually occurred around 11:00 in the morning, followed by a steep decline through the rest of the day and evening, but never a total cessation. Growth began to pick up again at about 2:00 in the morning, with a surge toward the midmorning peak. Puzzling this out, I realized that even with fully watered plants inside a greenhouse, the heat loads from direct summer sunlight could never be dissipated by transpirational cooling. On the average summer day, then, the factory closes its stomata pretty early, but opens them again in late evening. But how could these leaves be growing in pitch dark?

We have a traditional concept of growth as a single, integrated process, a factory with a single product. We try hard to be tolerant of other views of growth, but the expansion of a leaf or the increase of biomass is quite compelling. The plant itself does not share our interest in a single obvious growth process, relying instead on an ensemble of linked partial growth mechanisms.

One of these mechanisms, *carbon fixation*, requires reasonable temperatures, high ambient CO_2 levels, and open stomata to proceed. Fixation is indifferent to light or dark. Another partial process, *nutrient uptake*, requires open stomata, reasonable temperatures, and good soil moisture. It is also indifferent to light. *Photosynthesis*, the capture of light energy, requires light but is indifferent to temperature and water balance. *Sugar production* by the Calvin Cycle needs everything except light. All of these processes need energy, except photosynthesis, which produces it.

So it turns out that plant growth machinery is rarely idle. Except in periods of prolonged drought, cold, and darkness (e.g., Western Canadian winters) there is nearly always something to do.

Carbon fixation, nutrient uptake, photosynthesis, and sugar production are all major precursors to growth, but even growth itself is not a single process. *Cell division* is growth in theory, and can go on independent of sun or water, so long as photosynthate and reasonable temperatures are available. *Cell expansion* is growth in fact, the visible portion we are so keen to measure. It has its own set of specific requirements, namely a supply of recently-divided cells and a positive water balance, but is fairly indifferent to temperature and sunlight. So we arrive now at the basic heresy: plants need sunlight to manufacture the components for growth, but they don't need sunlight to grow.

Botanists, ecologists, and agronomists all search diligently for the single key parameter of plant development. Like industrial economists studying a factory, we look for some key integrator that best measures its performance. Volumes have been written, manifestations identified, methodology perfected, formulae promulgated and statistics prepared. But no single measurement of growth seems to hold sway very long. That early morning in the greenhouse taught me that a definition of plant growth is elusive.

We have all seen the time-lapse photography of the bean seedling unfolding, each frame showing the secret twists and turns as cotyledon leaves expand outward toward sunlight and destiny. But what we really need to visualize are the blurry instants between the stills.

Symbiosis

Don and Dorothy Swenson farm what is commonly known as a "sandpile," a belt of sandy land south of Moose Jaw, at the foot of the Missouri Coteau. Most of this land lost what little "A" horizon it had during the droughts and windstorms of the 1930s. The Swensons bought the land cheaply after the War and patiently began to restore it. The whole place is now divided into long, narrow, 40-acre fields. Dense caragana shelterbelts, planted broadside to the prevailing winds, divide each field. Early on, the Swensons realized that a mix of perennial crops would be essential to the management of this land, so they began to produce alfalfa seed in a rotation with certified wheat seed. This allowed them to minimize the amount of tillage, build the nitrogen and organic matter levels in the soil, and reduce the amount of fallow time to a negligible amount.

Next came leafcutter bees. Don and Dorothy first heard about these industrious little alfalfa pollinators from an Agriculture Canada entomologist at Lethbridge, and they decided to try them out. Management of the bees was complex; cocoons had to be imported every spring, held in controlled storage, and then released into the fields at just the right moment. Alfalfa seed yields increased dramatically with the leafcutters, and soon the Swensons figured out how to overwinter cocoons and produce a surplus for sale to other alfalfa seed producers.

Next came irrigation water. Don had read about an experiment in Vernon, British Columbia, where treated sewage effluent was used for agricultural irrigation. He knew that the city of Moose Jaw was faced with an expensive addition to their sewage treatment facility, so he spent the next *10* years working with the city, federal authorities, and his neighbors to get an effluent irrigation project going. The project, which covers several thousand acres, now runs like a Swiss watch. Moose Jaw civic authorities saved a bundle by not having to upgrade the sewage plant, and the Swensons plus several of their neighbors got bargain irrigation systems out of the deal.

The Swensons have mastered some rather profound bits of biology as they built their farm. In that sense, they are the farmers of one possible agricultural future, where management is focused on living and microbial systems, where recycling is not a frill but a serious undertaking, and where the land is not continuously besieged by chemical inputs and the heavy metal of large-scale tillage implements. I hope in some redesigned future there will be room, and a fair rate of return for their efforts, for farmers like the Swensons.

Perhaps the most strategic chunk of biology operating on this farm is symbiotic nitrogen fixation. Symbiosis is powerful. Whether the close mutual relationships come by lucky genetic fluke or by eons of mutual interest, they put both cooperating species at a competitive advantage. Blessed is the termite with his resident bacteria that digests the wood he eats; so the algae and fungus that together create the self-sustaining lichen; and so too the productive alfalfa-rhizobium association. There are many other examples of symbiosis, and still others yet to discover.

The essence of the legume-rhizobium association is found at the enzyme level. Non-leguminous plants, and man for that matter, are unable to directly tap the abundant and readily accessible source of nitrogen that is our atmosphere. They simply don't have an enzyme system able to capture and convert dinitrogen gas to a usable form.

Poor man: when he needs nitrogen to feed his crops, he has to resort to the crude and costly Haber process, in which air is heated to extreme temperatures to chemically convert nitrogen gas to nitrate. Then he hauls this corrosive substance to a warehouse, stores it, and at what he hopes is the appropriate time, spreads it on his field, considering himself lucky if his crop captures a mere quarter of what he puts on.

Non-leguminous plants are forced to scrounge around in the soil for the soluble nitrate and ammonia forms of nitrogen that are delivered in fertilizer, cast off by other organisms, washed in by runoff, or brought to earth by lightning. The ultimate irony is that man and the non-leguminous plants are immersed all the while in an atmosphere that is 79% nitrogen gas.

Now picture the legume symbiosis. Small swellings on the roots of legumes contain colonies of a special bacterium (*Rhizobium* sp.) that capture atmospheric nitrogen, convert it to nitrate, and feed it to the host plant in exchange for a tiny dribble of carbohydrate. No factories are needed, no warehouses, no transportation. Nothing leaks out, nothing is washed away. The bacteria work hard when the plant is at a growth stage that requires lots of nitrogen, and slow down when their host's needs taper off.

The development of this symbiosis has brought with it an elaborate specialization. The rhizobium that reads for the locoweed plant will wait patiently as a spore in the soil, ignoring the roots of a nearby vetch. An alfalfa rhizobium will have nothing to do with a lentil. Legume plants are divided into rhizobial cross-inoculation groups, just like humans can be divided into blood groups.

The legume family is full of bizarre and unique trace chemicals, and we are beginning to realize now that some of these are specialized "semiochemicals" (signal-conveying chemicals) that are released in root exudates to attract just the right strain of rhizobium.

Early agriculturalists knew intuitively that there was something special about legumes. They sought out the peas, the alfalfas, the beans, the lentils and so on, knowing they were plants of noble character, but not really knowing why. Long before the discovery of the symbiosis, a body of practical information grew up around the cultivation of legumes, particularly in the moister countries where native rhizobia can prosper and multiply in the soil.

The rhizobium symbiosis was discovered by a young Frenchman, Jean-Baptiste Boussingault (a student of the seminal German scientist, Alexander von Humboldt), in the 1880s. Boussingault proved legumes have special sources of nitrogen by showing they could grow in a nitrogen-free medium of crushed brick and distilled water.

Nodules, the root outgrowths that house the nitrogen-fixing bacteria, are curious structures. On some legumes they can be tiny, the size of a pinhead; on others they swell up to the size of a wad of chewing gum. The irregular shapes and deeply-cut lobes identify them as a plant organ that has been redirected and distorted by the presence of the bacteria. Some nodules look exactly like stumpy little hands.

The enzyme used by the bacteria to fix nitrogen will not function in the presence of oxygen, so the enclosing nodule serves to keep most air away from them. For backup, the bacteria also produce an oxygen-accepting molecule called leghemoglobin that removes the last of the oxygen from the nodule. This complex molecule differs in structure from the hemoglobin in human blood cells by only a single atom.

The agricultural industry has developed an elaborate system for ensuring that seeded legumes become infected by the correct nitrogen-fixing bacteria. Selected strains of rhizobium are mass-produced in industrial culturing systems, dried to a resting state, and packed for distribution. Farmers mix the inoculant with their seed, using a variety of ingenious application systems. Don Swenson adds a dribble of milk along with his inoculant, which ensures that the dusty black spore powder sticks firmly to the seed. A handful of inoculant will easily cover an acre.

The emerald green of the Swenson's alfalfa field is testimony to the effectiveness of this symbiosis. Nearby is another nodulated legume, caragana, that forms the massive windbreaks around Swenson's fields. Peas and beans run rampant in Dorothy's garden. Beyond the farm, on the nearby rangeland of the Missouri Coteau, are other legumes. Trailing vetch, buffalo bean, prairie clover, ground plum, locoweed and astragalus carefully husband their chosen bacteria.

A select handful of non-legumes have been able to devise similar nitrogen-fixing systems: the wolf willow of prairie rangelands, the buckbrush (*Cratageus* sp.) of British Columbia's ponderosa pine forests, and the widespread forest alder are three prominent examples.

The asset of nitrogen fixation makes certain legumes well suited as pioneer plants, or invaders into new soil. In the Great Sand Hills of west central Saskatchewan, the legume psoralea is one of the first plants to appear on a newly created dune. With a growth logic that goes well beyond the individual, psoralea colonizes a piece of ground, stabilizes it, and begins to contribute excess nitrogen, organic matter, shade, and stability to the abiotic and mineral sand. These activities soon make it possible for non-pioneer plant species to compete and gradually take over, squeezing out all but a few psoralea. This quirky legume is the first species of what will become, after many years of development, a mixed-grass prairie climax community.

Logging operations in British Columbia rely heavily on clovers to capture sites exposed from logging and road building. If the seeding is done properly, the clovers will prevent weed establishment, reduce erosion and provide nitrogen for companion grasses.

The Swensons have learned their biological lessons well, and this is no laid back, low energy farm, where nature "does its thing." Agriculture is a manipulative industry and the Swensons are active manipulators, but the inputs and systems they manipulate are primarily biological. Natural patterns and carefully conceived analogues of natural patterns are evident everywhere on the farm. The symbiosis they cultivate so carefully in their alfalfa is repeated on a larger scale in their own working partnership with the land.

The Grass and the Buffalo

Bison, bison. He is the ur-creature of Western North America: his flesh and blood are mingled with the very flesh and blood of this continent. Land, water, and flora were bent and shaped by him. He was the lord of the open western frontier. When that frontier closed, the living buffalo became a dying symbol. His time was from the last of the glaciers until the first of the white men. That era is like a distant symphony for us; we hear a phrase here, a chord there. When that music is finally reconstructed, buffalo is sure to be the coda.

Physical traces of his massive presence can still be seen.

Buffalo have a great need to rub, and on treeless prairie, the only objects tall and rigid enough for them were the rare boulder erratics, huge stones that somehow missed being pulverized by glaciers. Rubbing stones on rangeland became sacred sites, and paths converged on them from all points of the buffalo compass. (No one knows from how far they came.) The stones sit in deep, rounded depressions, the result of generations of animals working their way around them.

Geologists in the Dakotas puzzled for decades over some anomalous transverse slashes seen along ridges and river valleys. The slashes were gradually disappearing through cultivation, but aerial photographs of natural areas showed them extending over long distances. Explanations for the slashes ranged from glacial compression to seismic fault lines. Their very size and depth made it difficult to accept animal origin. But in the end, they were seen to be buffalo trails, braided heartlines across the palm of the land.

The size of the population at full flower will never be known. Frank Gilbert Roe, whose 1000-page book on the buffalo is a monument of obsessive scholarship, refuses to speculate. He does quote Ernest Thompson Seton's estimate of 50,000,000, a comfortable number. Roe also cites another observer, a Kansan from the mid 1800s, whose description puts the size of the buffalo population in perspective. The Kansan tells of a westward train trip that was held up for *three days* while a single migrating herd crossed the tracks.

Our buffalo were a conscious sacrifice. The entire history and ethos of North American settlement would have to be rewritten to accommodate their survival as wild animals. All that remains now are a few ranch herds, plus animal-park specimens in places like Moose Jaw and Calgary, where once the animal moved in imperial herds of 10,000. We keep the buffalo's image though, and it has powerful cultural overtones of wildness and independence. Buffalo is the ultimate doomed rebel.

Ranchers in the west have experimented with commercial buffalo herds over the years. The animal has a good feed conversion ratio, needs little care, and produces very lean meat.

But 10,000 years loose on the prairies have left their stamp. Corrals and holding pens must be made from telephone poles and two-by-tens. Calves that are tied up frequently kill themselves trying to get free. The genes for this wildness run deep: it takes two and three crosses with domestic cattle before the offspring – beefalo – are tractable.

Near the very end of the buffalo era, in the 1870s, prairie settlers collected buffalo bones for sale. One major shipping depot was just southeast of present day Regina, on the banks of Wascana Creek, at a place that became known as Pile o'Bones. Periodically the collected bones were loaded on freight cars and shipped east to be ground into fertilizer. Fuzzy photographs of this bone depot still exist. The neatly stacked bone piles stand out stark white alongside the dark freight cars and loading docks. The scene is strongly reminiscent of Dachau.

The pace of buffalo killing picked up dramatically at the end. Hunters, European tourists, fur traders, even Indians seemed desperately anxious to be rid of the great staggering buffalo enterprise, to put it out of its misery, perhaps. Many animals were shot for sport, their carcasses left untouched or with just the tongue removed.

During Sitting Bull's stay in southwestern Saskatchewan, it was U.S. military policy to intercept any northward-migrating herds and turn them back before they crossed into Canada, thus ensuring fatal separation of the Sioux from their sustaining buffalo.

The last Canadian buffalo herd was dispatched in 1878, but the American herds hung on a few years longer. The final curtain fell about 1891, in central Montana, when the last free-ranging herd was destroyed.

Individual animals remained – prairie rogues and small boreal forest groups. At their lowest ebb a few decades ago, the North American population stood at around 30,000. We have since pulled back from the brink to a captive population of roughly 100,000.

Buffalo grazed and rolled and trampled and dunged their way over this land for 10,000 years, and would have had a profound effect on our vegetation. The native grasses of buffalo range should be well adapted to these grazing animals, since we know that buffalo eat grass almost exclusively. Curiously though, many of our native grasses seem exquisitely sensitive to grazing of any kind.

If these grass species – the fescues, stipas, and wheatgrasses – evolved hand in hand with the shaggy buffalo, why then are they so fragile? Why do they decline so quickly under modern cattle grazing, to be replaced by other, less desirable vegetation?

The question forms a classic triangular problem, one of grazing, range grass physiology, and prehistoric buffalo herd movements. There are good intellectual dimensions to this question, from the practical all the way to the subcellular, and finally down the long sightline of paleontology. Some tentative answers are beginning to emerge.

Suppose there were four great regional buffalo herds. In late fall, horizons of midcontinental prairie turn pastel pink and blue, sloughs freeze hard, and the northern distances inspire melancholy. Forage is now mere wisps of dry grass, beaten by the wind. Individual bands of the first herd, the northern prairie herd, slowly rendezvous, reluctant to leave their chosen grassland. But finally they do leave, heading *north* to Canadian boreal forests or *west* to the sheltering foothills of the Rockies. Once in the forests, buffalo have shaken the cutting winds of winter prairie, and they can bed in insulating snow. Good forage – fescue and pinegrass – has grown there undisturbed all summer, and can be nosed out from under the snow. In the foothills, herds can water in streams that run all winter, instead of breaking ice or eating snow.

When spring calves come, herds move short distances, and melting snow uncovers more unused forage. The edge of the forest becomes a favored zone, providing the best of both worlds. The bugs are not bad yet, and the herds linger on in the forest. Finally, in full summer, prairie calls, and herds rumble past the Red Deers, Havres and Nipawins of the future, heading back to the center of the continent.

When they arrive, the cool-season stipas and wheatgrasses have already finished their period of rapid spring growth. Grazing would have little impact on them now, as they coast toward maturity and senescence. Meanwhile, the fescue grasses back in the foothills and parkland wintering areas have a chance to regrow undisturbed.

Suppose a second herd, this one summering in modern-day Montana and the Dakotas. As winter approaches, they move *southward* to the tall grasses and mild winters of the central plains. Here, in Kansas and Missouri, was the one part of the prairie that may have experienced season-long grazing. The tall-grass prairie of this area contained a large percentage of warm-season, C4 grasses. This was the Eurasia of the north American continent, the one place where summer and winter grazing may have overlapped, as various herds shifted in and out of the area.

A third regional herd might summer on the high plains along the eastern flanks of the Rockies, moving west into the foothills for winter.

Like geese in their flyways, these herds seem to have moved separately, each in its own broad and looping pattern of season and geography. Variations in a year's weather might cause the pattern to shift and rearrange, so no two migrations would be exactly alike. Still more variation would be introduced by the exact route a herd followed, and its selection of particular grazing and wintering places. Unfenced western north America was ideal terrain for random behavior. Herds may at times have simply flowed, the erstwhile leaders following their noses to the most immediate grass, shelter or sunlight.

Buffalo are very mobile. Wildlife biologists proved this by tracking a small captive herd in Yellowstone National Park. A technician would follow the herd quietly during the day and then make camp near them when they bedded down for the night. Time and again the technician would wake up at dawn to find the herd long gone, several miles away and moving fast.

When a big herd did stop to graze, chaos would reign. Grazing pressure was incredible; new leaves, old leaves, dead stems and seed heads were all either eaten or mashed into the ground. Shrubs were broken off and trampled. Vast quantities of manure and urine were laid down and the surface soil was thoroughly stirred up. In a very few days nothing edible would remain and the herd would leave. Then, because of the massiveness of the western space, three, five, even ten years might elapse before another herd would return to that same site.

How do we know this grazing pattern? We don't really. There is no ancestral evidence, no blurry photographs to study. Explorers' accounts from the middle and late 1800s described buffalo whose migrations were already profoundly disturbed. What conclusions we do have are the result of imaginative hypotheses and real conceptual daring. Scientists are uncomfortable with this kind of speculation, and use it only when confronted with deep complexity, as in the functioning of plant phloem, or in the case of minimal evidence. Historical buffalo migration is a classic case with no direct empirical evidence. The problem tweaked the interest of two archaeologists from Simon Fraser University in British Columbia. They confronted the migrations using a plant biochemistry tool called carbon dioxide isotope discrimination.

The carbon of atmospheric carbon dioxide has a normal atomic weight of 12. In the course of natural and cosmic events, a slightly different stable isotope is created, and there is a small, constant fraction of CO_2 in the atmosphere whose carbon has a weight of 13 instead of the normal 12. This is the mundane basis for what has become a wonderfully sensitive bioassay. Conventional cool-season grasses, with a C3 metabolic organization, recognize and discriminate between the two isotopes of carbon, and fix them into their tissues in a specific ratio to one another. Warm season, C4-metabolism grasses maintain a very different, but also constant, carbon isotope ratio. So constant are these ratios that they can be used as a chemical benchmark to distinguish between C3 and C4-type plant tissues.

The two SFU archaeologists saw that by using isotope discrimination analysis they could track the stable isotope carbon 13 as it wended its way through buffalo metabolism. The carbons fixed into the leaves of grasses are converted to the tissue and bone of grazing animals, still maintaining their appropriate isotopic ratio. Thus bone tissue of grazers living in C4-dominated southern prairie would have a very different carbon 13/carbon 12 ratio than bone from more northern grazing animals that lived on a strict C3 diet.

The researchers collected ancestral bison bone from various

sites in the Alberta foothills. Their hypothesis was that these bones should have a ratio typical of cool season C3 grasses, since those types are dominant in the foothills and the northern prairies. Sure enough, the opposite, null hypothesis was proven: the bone carbon ratio was intermediate between C4 and C3 diets. So the buffalo cycled, the scientists concluded, between northern C3 forest and southern C4 prairie.

North American rangeland needs a consumer, we know that much. Protect a site from use for 15 years or so and it gets rank with dead material. Grass growth is restricted, snow mold becomes a problem, and soils stay cold far into the spring. We know the indigenous consumers were buffalo, grasshoppers, and fire, but we don't know how to replace them.

Ten thousand years allowed the grass and the buffalo time to develop a subtle biogeographical transaction. The grasses arranged their geographical locations and their life cycles in a way that minimized use during growth and maximized it during dormancy. The buffalo, for their part, guaranteed that when they did graze a site they would do it aggressively, indiscriminately, briefly, and rarely. All of the manure and urine generated at that site was returned to it and churned into the soil, along with seeds and litter. There was no hundred percent guarantee to the grazing transaction, but it was just consistent enough for both grazed and grazer to shape their lives and gene pools to it.

Seasonal grazing was unique to the New World; the Old World ranges in the Altai, the Caucasus, and Turkestan were used year around, and domestic herding started there thousands of years sooner than in North America. The grasses of those regions – brome, crested wheatgrass, cheatgrass, among others – could not escape their grazers, and were forced to perform growth and reproduction in their presence. Thus the annual cycles of many Old World grasses are brief explosions of vegetative growth in early spring, followed by a race to flowering and senescence. Seeds are programmed to germinate quickly; life cycles are compressed from months down into weeks, and their engines of growth run on a very lean mixture of water and nutrients. Genes are programmed for maximum leaf and minimum root.

Cunning Canadian botanists of the early 1900s traveled to these places and recognized their unique grazing environments. When they returned home, battered suitcases disgorged packets of seed they had collected. The performance of these introduced grasses on the prairie research stations – Swift Current, Manyberries, Lethbridge – was stunning. The crested wheatgrasses and Russian wild ryes could germinate, grow, and hold down soil in the harsh dustbowl. Prairie Farm Rehabilitation agronomists, real heroes of the dirty thirties, traveled to hundreds of farmer meetings, one driving while the other one slept, to spread the gospel of these grasses. Thousands and thousands of eroding wheat fields were planted with crested wheatgrass and saved from further destruction.

But the season of crested will never suit the ghosts of departed buffalo, and thus it remains an alien on North American range. The ground in between crested plants gradually becomes bare and sterile. No other vegetation develops. The tough and wiry crested seed stalks begin to accumulate, leaving no room for new leaf growth. Roots break down quickly, leaving little stable organic matter in the soil.

Crested does fit the needs of our domestic cattle, in one special instance. In early spring they can be turned onto crested pasture to feed on its prodigious early growth, while leaving the native pasture to the spring rest it is accustomed to.

What about the fourth great north American buffalo herd, the one that would have grazed on the vast resources of intermountain bluebunch wheatgrass west of the Rockies? It simply did not exist. Historical evidence speaks only of small and very occasional groups of buffalo in the entire intermountain region. The Cascade rain shadow apparently held the level of grass growth and drinking water to below the needs of the buffalo, and perhaps the mountain ranges made the spaces too confining. So the Pacific Northwest Grasslands coevolved with aridity, solitude, and the occasional deer, antelope, and elk, but no buffalo. Therein may lie the exquisite sensitivity of bluebunch wheatgrass to grazing.

For a few decades, this bluebunch grass carried a good portion of the early western cattle industry and the quirky subculture that went with it. But the bluebunch has given way, gradually but profoundly, to the invading cheatgrass, another Eurasian alien. Now bluebunch is a pathetic remnant, and cheatgrass dominates some 40,000,000 acres of its original range. Knapweed, a thistle-like European broadleaf, commands another 2,000,000.

The old trails and rubbing stones mark one of the world's great migration cycles. The buffalo niche remains, tenanted awkwardly by our grain and cattle, but the living presence of the wild animal is no longer with us. There is a residue of its spirit though. When I get far enough away from the grid roads and wheat fields, I sense a buffalo-energy in this land, running from calving ground, through trail and salt lick, to buffalo pound and rubbing stone. As long as we retain some native prairie, that energy will remain.

The Hellbender at the Bottom of the Dugout and Other Acquaintances

Reptiles and amphibians form part of the biological landscape of Western Canada, even though our list of species is relatively small. Frogs, snakes, turtles, toads, salamanders, and even lizards pursue their cold-blooded destinies here. These animals are essentially desert and tropical lifeforms. North American distribution maps of reptile species show a high degree of concentration and overlap in southern California, and the amphibian species congregate heavily in the Gulf states. The very existence of Canadian genera makes them interesting. The 49th parallel is a totally artificial boundary, but it is a real boundary in the West in two ways: it tracks the southern extent of continental glaciation, and it is close to the northern limit of range for nearly all reptiles and amphibians. Frogs are the one exception. They are everywhere, giving rise to the folklore that they get sucked up into the sky and redistributed in the rain.

Reptiles and amphibians also inhabit another landscape, that of the human psyche.

We are fascinated by these creatures. The fascination may take the form of repulsion, but it is a fascination nonetheless. We contemplate the scales, the warty skin, and the unblinking eyes across a frightening biological gulf. These are the bright students that long ago dropped out of evolutionary school and went bad, to the point of developing fangs and venom. They inhabit our dreams and occasionally our basements. We celebrate them in folklore and sexual mythology. Many psychologists have tried to come to grips with our feelings about reptiles and amphibians.

Arthur Koestler proposed that part of our human brain (the violent part) is unevolved and reptilian, so we might be looking at these species as the embodiment of our own worst instincts.

I have a simpler explanation. It has to do with overlapping niche.

The young of our own species spend a lot of time foraging in and around sloughs, storm channels, gravel pits, dugouts, and so on. These same habitats include very visible and catchable populations of reptiles and amphibians. From simple niche overlap comes a long tradition of slippery afternoons, muddy sneakers, and squirming prizes brought home for the exquisite disgust of all. Kids and especially frogs grow up together, sharing the rich and muddy "waste places" that adults avoid.

Beyond this bond of niche, there is also something compelling in the momentary possession of these wild things, so unlike ourselves. As a kid in southern California, I was subject to this fascination for a rather extended period. For a time I specialized in snakes. My friend David Myers and I once bought a five-foot indigo snake at a pet store. He owned the front half and I owned the back, and we shared the responsibilities of keeping it. Captive snakes are notoriously picky eaters, and this one was no exception. We offered it everything from mice to raw hamburger until we found that it liked eating day-old cockerels, which were free at a local hatchery. We time-shared the snake and when my time was up, I would drape the animal around my neck and carry it through the neighborhood to David's house. The panic it created was balm to my herpetological ego.

At one time I had half a dozen cages in my bedroom, each containing some precious and necessary beast. I became expert, an artist, in the ways of the alligator lizard. I knew just what rotten boards to look under, and how to catch them so they would not drop their long, graceful tails. My mother was very patient.

The childhood fascination wore off, but a strong affinity carried through to adulthood. Walking across Regina's Albert Street Bridge one day, I spotted a turtle sunning itself on the banks of Wascana Lake, and the old reptilian bond stirred again. Seeing the turtle reminded me there was more to the cold-blooded fauna of Western Canada than plain old garter snakes, which are ultimately boring, and smelly besides.

I wasn't able to get close to the turtle, but after the sighting I began to watch sloughs and creeks more closely, hoping to get a closer look, or even to catch one momentarily. My chance came when one of the local kids told me there was a turtle in the storm channel near our suburban house.

This storm channel is a minor unnamed tributary of Wascana Creek, with its headwaters near the Canadian Tire store. The city parks department has straightened the channel and graded the banks to a perfect, engineered V-shape. All shoreline vegetation is ruthlessly eliminated, the channel is sprayed regularly with herbicides and insecticides, and the water level changes frequently. In short, it is a lousy environment for nearly anything to live in, let alone turtles, which are notoriously fussy. I figured the kids were fooling me, playing on a known weakness. Why would a turtle want to live among the shipwrecked grocery carts, beer bottles, styrofoam cups, abandoned bicycles, supermarket flyers, and carwash discharge of a suburban storm channel? But sure enough he was there, a Western Painted turtle with the green, yellow, and orange face markings characteristic of the species.

The turtle stayed just inside the upstream end of a road culvert. If the coast was very clear, he would venture just beyond the lip of the pipe and you could see his slow, rhythmic dogpaddle. I carefully floated a disabled grasshopper past him once, but he would have none of it.

A turtle that wary would never willingly choose a narrow and exposed storm channel as a home, I knew. We decided he must have been captured at a lake somewhere and brought back to the city by some fast-fingered kid. After the novelty and the screams wore off, the kid likely hit on the expedient of dumping the turtle into the nearby storm channel, not bothering about the niceties of turtle habitat preference.

We watched the turtle off and on for two weeks, until a good rain came and swelled the storm channel. When the water went back down he was gone, carried off, I suppose, into mother Wascana.

What a lovely, cagey beast he was, and worthy of our bond of fascination! Ecologically, turtles are something like eagles: highly specialized, requiring lots of territory, and sitting at the apex of a vulnerable food chain. A body of water that supports turtles is a stable, complex environment. Notable sites for the Western Painted turtle are the Kootenay Marsh near Creston,

British Columbia, the Qu'Appelle Lakes of Saskatchewan, and the southern end of Lake Winnipeg in Manitoba.

Turtle shows up as an icon in many cultures down through time, as fascination is built into myth. The Plains Indians took turtle as a symbol of wisdom, and paid homage to it with monuments of placed stones. One of their turtle figures is found near Minton, on the Saskatchewan-North Dakota border. Fortunately it is at the top of a hill, on grazing land that is too rough to farm. In the center of the turtle's carapace is a round cairn, joined to the head and tail by a narrow stone midline. The figure is 45 meters across.

The negative side of the bond between men and reptiles is repulsion and conscious unknowing. In the Grasslands National Park area near the southern Saskatchewan town of Val Marie, there is a single site where the prairie rattlesnake is found. Accessible only on foot, the den is miles away from the nearest farmhouse, and the snakes pose no threat to the odd range cow that might wander across the steep and eroded landscape. Yet people feel the need to hunt these snakes down; a visitor to the dens frequently finds empty shotgun shells lying about. The fact that these tropical cold-blooded animals have found a niche in the badlands of Saskatchewan should be cause for sympathetic interest rather than fear.

The tiger salamander is another denizen of the West, a slough and pond-dwelling amphibian, found (ironically) in the Palliser Triangle and the Okanagan valleys.

My first encounter with the salamander was on a deserted prairie grid road. He was crossing from a dry slough to a wet one, and he was totally intent. His walk was crude, a barely modified swim. First his body would arc to the right, throwing the left forelimb forward. Then the right rear leg would come forward. Then the two cocked legs would together give a mighty shove, moving him a little farther across the road. Then his body would arc to the left, and the process would start over again. He looked as if he might forget the correct sequence at any minute.

This salamander was simply leaving a dry slough in search of a wet one, but he was also re-enacting an earlier emergence, that of his dinosaur ancestors as they moved onto dry land. Imagine what a shock the prehistoric world must have had when this little beast's ancestor first crawled dripping from the swamps, all slimy and glistening, its beady yellow eyes surveying new territories to conquer.

I picked up the midget dinosaur and he continued his thrashing, side-to-side walk in midair. This was an adult: his head was triangular and almost snakelike. Immature salamanders are totally aquatic and have a spongy set of gills behind the head. There are stories, folklore really, of giant salamanders that stay permanently in the juvenile stage and reach enormous size. Hellbenders, they are called. These aberrations grow quietly in the bottom of the dugout, like a nightmare, taking ducks and eyeing children.

Salamanders are unique in the vertebrate world in their ability to commit parthenocarpy, which is the ultimate biological sin of procreation without sex. It is thought that parthenocarpy is an adaptive option in disturbed environments, since a successful individual mutation could produce cloned offspring. Indeed, salamanders are the reverse of turtles and seem to tolerate high levels of pollution and disturbance.

I carried that salamander, my antithesis, my latter-day sexless dinosaur, across the grid road and dropped him into a permanent slough. He swam off ungrateful and uncaring, but I was happy. I had renewed our bond of association.

There are other saurian personalities I have yet to see first-hand, like the snapping turtles of the Souris River, the tiny horned toads (actually lizards) of Georgovia, Saskatchewan, the smooth green snake of Manitoba, the Pacific treefrog and western skink of southern British Columbia. There is something pure and clean about reptiles and amphibians in this country: they are not pests, they have no real economic value, they are just *there* as quirky and vastly distant lifeforms. And they are not abundant: even in ideal and unspoiled habitats, you have to look closely for them.

Perhaps if we can keep our turtles, green snakes, and skinks, and realize that to preserve them is to preserve their habitat, we will have achieved a sort of wisdom.

Roy LaMotte's Cows

Every spring a minor side-valley of the Okanagan would be invaded by a herd of 300 dusty, bawling, Hereford cows. The valley's back-to-the-landers would rush to protect their gardens, and whole families of orchardists would turn out to keep the herd away from their trees. Newly arrived retirees would phone the police. For the most part the cattle were content to go up the valley road, but not always.

Roy LaMotte, the owner of these cattle, never spoke about the damage these drives up the valley might cause, but I know he felt guilty about it. He rode straight up the road, shoulders set, not looking left or right, and leaving me, the younger buck, to retrieve errant heifers from backyards and herb gardens.

This daylong drive was a ranch tradition started before Roy was born, when the road was just a rutted horse track and the valley's only inhabitants were a miner or two.

I certainly felt guilty as the offended residents glared at me, a landless back-to-the-lander making do as a hired man. But I did love the drives, when we took the cattle from their spring range in the valley up to summer range in the mountains. Roy knew right where to push the cows, and every year we would come up out of the valley by a different route, landing always on some south-facing, open slope that was belly-deep in pine-grass.

As we rested the horses and ate cold sandwiches, we would watch the cattle. Roy's interest was proprietary; mine was in anything to do with cattle ranching. The cows would be hungry after a whole day without food, and would keep their heads buried deep in the grass. They would clamp down on a mouthful and, with a quick side-to-side shake of the head, rip leaves and stems from the sward. Two or three quick chews would follow, a step, and then another ripping bite. With no sound other than the swish of hooves through the sward, the ripping and chewing of 300 hungry animals was almost deafening.

Roy was a first-class grazing manager. He knew the range, and maintained sufficient curiosity over the years to keep adding to his stock of knowledge. When I knew him, he could look back on 40 or 50 springs worth of snowmelts, late frosts and grass greenup. He couldn't have been called a gentle man, but he was always considerate of his cattle and horses, in contrast to some of the other district cattlemen. And, in his own un-schooled way, he was painfully aware of the contradictions of a traditional cattle drive through a modern hippie refuge.

Roy was not a "manager" in the modern agricultural sense. He simply orchestrated and fine-tuned an ancient natural process. He was a grazier, a transhumant, a rangeman; he would have trouble putting the essence of his job into words. If asked, his answer would probably be "looking after cattle," but in his best moments he was looking after the grass.

North American grasslands had 10,000 years to co-evolve with buffalo, elk, deer and antelope; in most cases they have had less than a hundred years' experience with the cow. The fit is pretty good on cultivated grasslands and generally terrible on native grasslands.

Domestic cattle are lazy. Rarely do they graze more than a kilometer or two away from water sources, they avoid rough terrain, they don't like to climb hills, and they tend to regraze the same plants over and over rather than seeking out new forage. The typical destructive cattle-range scenario runs like this: a large tract of fenced land, traditionally grazed from May to September, is seen to be in deteriorating condition. The manager responsible does the obvious and, prior to the May turnout, he reduces the number of cows allowed on that range. The cattle start their grazing season around the watering facility, spending a lot of time in the shade of nearby willows or poplars. All the newly grazed grass comes back green and handy. Meanwhile, more distant and less accessible grass grows unhindered and begins to mature. The repeatedly grazed grasses struggle to maintain productive leaf surface by sacrificing root growth. Soil water uptake is reduced. The grass becomes less competitive and soon unpalatable weedy species begin to move in. Meanwhile more distant grass stands have gone into maturity largely untouched. Dry leaves and stems of these ungrazed plants stay upright, shading out the new growth underneath. Like the overgrazed plants, overmature plants also grow weaker, although at a slower rate. Two or three years of this and the grazing manager will be at wits' end. Stocking rate is well below normal, yet the pasture continues to run down.

This scenario is sickeningly familiar all over the western North American range. It is based on an imperfect understanding of grass dynamics, and the difference between the cow and buffalo economy.

Ideally, native range should be grazed intensively for short periods of time, starting in midsummer. When the cattle are turned out, they need to be crowded to the point that they are competing for forage and grazing non-selectively. Then, after some precise length of time (which no one has yet been able to quantify), the stock must be rotated onto another pasture, allowing the first one several weeks (or months, or even years) of rest before it is grazed again in a similar fashion.

This regime, crudely analogous to a buffalo grazing economy, poses a real challenge to the rangeman. How does he create these pastures, with fences and appropriate water, when the land can only return a few dollars an acre at best? Alternatively, where does one find a herdsman in a society bent on churning out color commentators and management accountants?

Roy's profession as a rangeman is a curious blend of the non-technical and laid back together with detailed local knowledge and constant observation of grass, seasons, soil, livestock, game, fences, and water. Even professional range researchers do much of their work with simple grass clippers, a drying oven, a scale, and a calculator.

Range management is a schizophrenic profession. Grizzled ranchers like Roy tend to show up at research conferences wearing business suits, and the researchers frequently arrive

wearing Levis and chewing snoose. It is a good sign when the
scientists and the workers of a particular profession are suffi-
ciently attracted to each other that they cross-dress.

Canada, one of the great range countries of the world, has
virtually ignored the discipline of range management. No
Canadian university offers even an undergraduate degree in
the subject, and there are only a handful of professionals
working in the field. Yet the issues are profound, and the
questions fascinating.

One researcher performed a series of experiments to find if
cow saliva, left on the cut edge of a grass blade, had any kind of
a hormonal growth-promoting effect on the plant. And whether
buffalo saliva differed in activity from cow saliva.

Another researcher followed sheep as they grazed, and
found they tended to orient to one another in a particular way.
Sheep eye orbits are about 60 degrees apart, and as a flock
slowly disperses across a pasture each animal will try to
maintain a neighbor in sight at that angle – that is, one at 30
degrees either side of straight ahead. That way the animals can
keep their heads down and graze and still link themselves to an
early warning network.

Others have pursued the interaction of cattle and wild elk.
Elk actually prefer range lightly grazed by cattle to ungrazed
range, but will reject heavily-grazed cattle range.

The field-scale grazing of Roy's Herefords on Okanagan
pinegrass can be scaled down to defoliation (leaf removal) on a
single plant basis, for a clearer understanding of what actually
happens. Grass leaves grow linearly, pushing up from the
bottom, rather than expanding all along the periphery as most
plant leaves do. This adaptation prevents the meristem (the

growing point) from being grazed off. If a cow nips off an emerging grass blade, the remaining leaf still gets to finish its growth. The meristem of most broadleaved plants is near the top of the plant; when it is grazed off, growth must start over somewhere else.

Grass leaves emerging after defoliation or grazing are smaller, denser, more prostrate, and higher in chlorophyll content than their predecessors. This finding has led many to speculate on the theory of "compensatory growth," that grazing-adapted plants actually become more efficient as they are grazed. This notion has all the hallmarks of Einstein's personal scientific "themata," ideas that catch hold of certain researchers and will not let them go. Some tantalizing evidence for compensatory growth does exit, but the idea is a hostage of our still imperfect understanding of grass growth.

Nomadic grazing in North Africa has long been identified as a destructive practice, but now more and more we are coming to recognize that traditional North American stationary grazing is also destructive. Paradoxically, we stock our ranges with too few cattle, for too long a time.

The buffalo and North America's native grasses had 10,000 years to get to know each other's habits. Range managers have worked cows over western North America in most instances for less than a century. So far no one knows for sure what constitutes correct cattle grazing philosophy on native grass. The agendas of conferences like those of the Society for Range Management are crammed full of research papers on the topic.

Larger social issues are emerging on the range as well: do cattle belong in wilderness and protected areas, is red meat healthy, and is cattle production environmentally sustainable? These are big questions that will take time to resolve. I see an unfortunate willingness to divide into opposing and mutually exclusive camps on issues like these, and wonder if the greatest item at stake here is not threatened livelihoods or a degrading environment, but our increasing willingness to abandon any common social agendas.

Perhaps the only thing we can say now for sure is that the correct range management philosophy, whatever it may turn out to be, will mean nothing unless it is applied by canny and patient individuals like Roy LaMotte.

The Hole in the Glacier

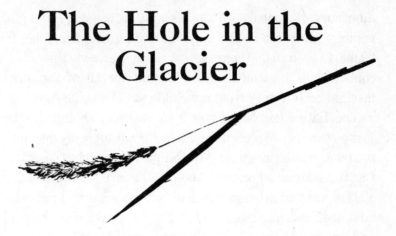

We Canadians like landscapes, and every summer we spend millions of dollars traveling around to look at them. These scenic tours can only be taken in the present, though, and that is a great pity. Wouldn't it be wonderful to navigate through the carboniferous swamps of Pre-Cambrian Saskatchewan, drive through the tropical forests of ancient Baffin Island, or send postcards from the Rocky Mountain erogeny?

Not being able to go myself, I collect re-creations of these prehistoric landscapes. Museums sometimes have good paintings and dioramas, but the really classic images are found in children's illustrated dinosaur books. In these, if you look beyond the battling Tyrannosaurs, you can see everything – smoking volcanoes, grotesque plants, vast and fetid swamps, bizarre mountain ranges. I look on those picturebook images with something akin to lust.

The ancient landscape I think I would most like to visit is mid-north America in the late Pleistocene, long after the dinosaurs disappeared. Paleontology, archaeology and glacial geology intersect in this tiny chunk of geological time, from 30,000 to about 9,000 years ago. A classic period in the life of our continent, it is a legitimate claimant for all of the surplus fascination left over from my childhood Dinosaur Age.

The Late Pleistocene was a curious and changeable time, just on the cusp of recorded history, simultaneously ancient and modern. At the beginning of the period, nearly the whole of Canada stagnated under 20,000,000 square kilometers of glacial ice, with an average depth of half a kilometer. The ice sheet advanced and retreated at least three times during the period, and by the end the whole thing had melted to a mere pittance. Agassiz, the resulting lake, became the biggest in world history, and then shrank to mere Lake Winnipeg. Midcontinent became tundra, then spruce forest, and finally a new phenomenon, prairie, began to emerge. Three great glacial valleys had been scoured out and the Okanogan, Kootenay and Columbia rivers emerged to fill them. Hordes of large mammal species mysteriously disappeared. The Bering Land Bridge surfaced as a cold cycle froze additional seawater, drawing ocean levels down. The Bridge disappeared under meltwater as the climate swung back again, but not before shadowy human figures crossed it, heading eastward.

The Late Pleistocene is essentially a lost memory to us, one that begs re-creation. First entry, the loss of those large mammals, the glaciers, and the dynamic landscapes are all part of a New World identity. We need that human memory, even if it must be constructed mainly from Carbon 14 and imagination.

Aboriginal cultures did not record first entry in either history or mythology. Paleontologists assume that humans first came to North America sometime during the late Pleistocene, but estimates of the date of first entry vary widely and provoke argument. Focusing so much research attention on the arrival is curious, but there is definitely something in us that responds strongly to this idea of entry into a new and empty continent. Arriving in what is now Alaska forever fixed a past heritage, and a future worldview. When the new entrants first stepped onto this continent, they exercised their first option in the New World and the last one, for a long time, that had any limitations attached to it.

Here was the ultimate experience, the one our human psyche is probably most suited for: new land, pure adventure, unlimited consumption, and constant movement. Although it may not have seemed so at the time, the first entrants had unrestricted freedom in a new environment. It would have been like a dream sequence, full of great personal significance. Welcome to the great empty hotel of the New World.

Glaciers, the great gray eminences of the Pleistocene, have made our research into the era very difficult. In addition to building and destroying landscapes on a continental scale, glaciers also took most of the paleontological evidence and scrambled it into mush. North American archaeologists have quite a time of it as a result. In Africa and unglaciated central Europe, deeper means older. Not here. With one or two notable exceptions, the North American new and old have been relentlessly ground together.

One of those exceptions is Old Crow, a major archaeological site in the Yukon, near the Alaska border. Miraculously, the site was unglaciated, and human artifacts from it have been reliably dated at 28,000 years BP (before the present). I think of Old Crow as the North American jump-off place, a base camp where the new immigrants paused, heard stories and sharpened their courage. The cold would have been abysmal, far colder than the Yukon of today. But then these new entrants were a people comfortable with their previous life in the Russian arctic.

The first migrating wave (there appear to have been several) paused for a time at Old Crow, because the very conditions that produced the Bering land bridge would have sealed most of the North American continent with inhospitable glacial ice. But central Alaska and the northwestern Yukon formed an ice-free refugium, unglaciated not because of any warmth, but from extreme dryness. Some time later the climate warmed again, the Bridge disappeared, and melting caused a narrow seam to appear in the glacier. This seam was actually the dividing line between the massive Laurentide glacier to the east and the Cordilleran to the west. The seam ran roughly southeastward, following the border between present-day Yukon and the Northwest Territories, down the eastern slope of the Rockies and into eastern Montana, which was the southern limit of glaciation.

One scientist conceptualized the climatic control of land bridge and glacier as the "Yukon lock." Conditions that opened the upstream (Bering) end of the lock closed the downstream (glacial seam) end, and vice versa. Old Crow sat midway between the locks. One of the favored activities in Old Crow appears to have been cracking mastodon bones for their marrow. This probably helped pass a strange and fearful time in the lock.

What induced the new entrants down the newly opened seam is not known. Certainly the going would have been difficult, over new moraines and fast-moving water. The corridor could have been very narrow, perhaps with both glaciers in view at times.

Spilling out of the seam into open Montana country must have been a profound experience for these first paleo-Indians, but curiously, they did not stop. There is a near vacuum of any first-wave archaeological evidence between Old Crow and Mexico City, which means these people shot straight through, never settling until they reached Central and South America.

Was it fear, the joy of movement, or the desire for hot climates that drove these people all the way through North America to the South American jungles? One theory put forward to explain this anomaly suggests that the first migrant group had originally occupied warmer climates in present-day China. They were forced northward to Beringia, and eventually across the Land Bridge, by hostile groups pushing up from the south. When they hit the New World, they kept going until the tropical climate of Mesoamerica tugged at their memories.

Whatever their motivation, these originals settled and went on to build the splendid Aztec, Toltec, Mayan, Chibchan, and Incan civilizations.

After the first wave came a long, profound pause. The new Central and South American societies saw no further influx of migrants, and went on to establish a genetic identity quite separate from later North American groups.

Some 15,000 years later, coincident with another opening and closing of the Yukon lock, a second wave of immigrants moved onto the continent. This second group had two migratory options, due to the further shrinkage of the glaciers: move southward along the traditional corridor, or eastward along the now unglaciated Arctic coast. They did both. Those who traveled east differentiated into the Inuit cultures. Those who turned south gave us the rich and continuing tapestry of the North American Indian. The First Ones, grandchildren of

Siberians, became grandparents in their time to the Assiniboine, the Nez Percé, the Seminole, the Zuni, the Cree.

What pure adventure. The aboriginals exploded down through that glacial funnel into a warm, rich, and totally unknown environment, and made it their own. The much-touted European exploration of North America, aided by friendly guides and powerful technologies, looks mean by comparison.

The logic of the glaciers meant that the first immigrants to the Canadian prairies came there by way of Beringia, Old Crow, Edmonton, Montana, and the Dakotas. Northward, eastward, pause, southward, and then northward again, into newly-exposed Canadian landscapes. A complex and graceful migratory curve. I would like to have been there.

Somewhere in this same Pleistocene era, the continent lost quite a bestiary of large mammals. Even the short list is impressive: mastodon, woolly mammoth, short-faced bear, ground sloth, superbison, saber-tooth tiger. The scale of some of these animals is daunting: superbison standing three meters high at the shoulder, the short-faced bear big enough to dwarf a grizzly. (One theory has it that the short-faced bear was so formidable that it kept humans from penetrating southward into its domain until it became extinct.)

What happened to these animals? Why did the fabulously successful sabertooth disappear from North America in a geological instant? Why the mammoth? In Europe, man coexisted for tens of thousands of years with mammoth, but here in the New World, the species disappeared almost overnight.

When confronted with a research problem, even a difficult one, few scientists start from scratch, rewriting disciplinary canons to fit the dimensions of a problem. Instead, we take confirmed and accepted theories and assemblages of facts to build bridges into the unknown territory. If, midway through construction of such a bridge, flaws are discovered in a major girder or foundation, the tendency is to patch and go on, rather than to start over and redesign based on the new information. Something similar happened in our research on the Pleistocene.

Early work on the North American late Pleistocene dated first human entry as very recent, and megafaunal extinctions as very old. Then a rash of discoveries occurred, pushing radiocarbon-verified dates of human occupation back further and further. Radiocarbon was to archaeology as fiberglass was to the pole vault: they both changed record books by quantum amounts.

I vividly remember the discovery of the Marmes site, a cave alongside the Columbia River where human habitation was dated at a record-breaking 9,000 years; archaeologists worked feverish 24-hour shifts to finish their excavations before the U.S. Army Corps of Engineers flooded the site with another dam, allowing us to live even better, electrically. That was in the late 1960s; other, older sites soon passed it by and Marmes is now a paleontological footnote.

As the date of earliest human occupation went spinning off into the past, one scholar made the simple observation that the era of humans and the era of North American megafauna now overlapped. Paul Martin, a perceptive archaeologist from the University of Arizona, went to work on that overlap, and in 1973 came up with a stunning theory that demolished the bridge, and still creates shock waves nearly 20 years later.

The traditional assumption was that wild climate swings of the late Pleistocene caused the demise of the large mammals. Humans had nothing to do with it. A temperate climate and forested habitat under the shadow of the glacier favored the existence of these beasts, and they simply weren't able to cope with the altithermal, a warm period at the end of the Pleistocene. But this explanation left some holes. What about the many other, smaller Pleistocene forest creatures that did survive the altithermal? What about the buffalo and the moose? Why did the megafauna disappear so suddenly, when the great continental forests staggered and crashed over thousands of years?

Martin proposed a radical answer. Yes, he said, the favored moist forest habitat was becoming restricted during the altithermal, and more animals crowded into what was left. Just as this was happening though, some wild-eyed newcomers popped out of a hole in the glacier. These second-wave migrants descended on the partly-glaciated midcontinent like Hells Angels on a church picnic: fast, destructive, and unexpected. The megafauna, trapped and unable to respond, were fairly easy prey for the organization and flint-bladed throwing spears of the new arrivals.

Mid-America was an unexploited paradise for a resourceful group whose *vitae* included Beringia, Old Crow, the glacial seam, and possibly the short-faced bear. They literally exploded, said Martin, moving from one kill site to another, rarely stopping, and experiencing very high birth rates. Martin proposed a "killing front" of scattered bands that radiated southward in an accelerated hunt/migration, covering the continent, from Edmonton to the Gulf of Mexico, in some 300 years. The megafauna never recovered from this killing wave, and stumbled on to extinction.

The vision of restless, efficient hunters in the midst of unwary animals and changing landscape rings true. Human movements to and from North America have always been associated with faunal extinctions. Martin's theory has a classic New World stink of reality about it.

I envy Paul Martin's sense of the Pleistocene. His childhood must have been steeped in lurid dinosaur books. Not only did he recreate that ancient landscape in detail, but he also provided a mechanism to make it work.

The Forest Cycle

The prairie cycle is complete now, in spite of many corners left
unvisited, and many projects left undone. My 15 years there
add to an ongoing sum of place experience, and the region is
now truly a landscape of the mind. Writers often claim that
distance from a place of strong attachments is useful in writing
about that place. When we move, one part of our consciousness
begins recasting the experiences of our past place while the
rest carries on with the daily business of the new.

A new cycle has started in the forests and valley grasslands
of British Columbia's southern interior. I have dozens of verti-
cally stratified ecologies to learn, from sagebrush valley bottoms through complex gradations of forest to alpine meadows,
and I have the infinite delight of place-discovery to look forward to. The painful and humbling part is learning species. An
aging memory system is complaining bitterly about having to
learn tree taxonomy.

The cycle is well along. In April I was able to take extensive night walks through gently enfolding Kootenay forests, while the prairies were still in the grip of dying winter. The spring air was moist and nearly tactile, and the cottonwoods smelled of strong honey. In my better moments, I feel stirrings of the same landscape compulsion that came to me so strongly in the sagebrush many years ago.

Already I see that this is a more inward landscape of shorter vistas and darkened understories. Ragged morning mists cling to forested hillsides, reluctant to leave. The land becomes open and explicit only when seen from ridges and peaks.

I wonder about the rock; it is everywhere, asserting itself, surging out of the ground, blocking passage. Whole mountains can be one continuous slab. Hidden in rock's massive darkness lie precious distillations of the earth's substance, and its secrets are not given up easily. Solitary miners commune with veins and outcroppings, chipping and probing, listening for any anomalies in vibration. Some valleys are gated at their lower ends by massive rock walls that force the creek or river through a narrow gorge. Inevitably, access roads get cut through these barriers, but there is a strong sense of intrusion as one crosses them.

Even in the depths of this mountain forest, there are openings that contain plant species common to the prairies. Fields of glacial till in valley bottoms produce soil profiles reminiscent of Saskatchewan. And these great upwellings of metamorphic rock crumble and shatter, in a continuous sacrifice to valley, delta, and ultimately, prairie.

The process of that sacrifice is elaborate. An errant lichen spore might come to rest on a bare granite slab. Minute amounts of dissolved nutrients lie on the surface of the slab, nourishing the lichen, and helping it establish itself. Soon the rock underneath is etched and pitted by organic acids released by the lichen. Club moss takes over from the lichen, and pine needles accumulate. The rockface underneath now stays wet for long periods, and a small crack appears. Winter freezes water in the crack, widening it minutely. A wandering ponderosa pine root finds the crack and relentlessly forces its way in. Summer sun heats the rock unevenly, and temperature differential finally causes a triangular chunk to shear off. It bounces down the slab to come to rest in a talus funnel, which collects all the rockfall from the mountain face above. Every spring the rocks in the funnel grind against each other, moving downslope with the runoff and the weight of new rock being added from the crumbling mountain. By the time the triangular rock reaches its destination creek, the sharp angles are gone.

The pounding of spring breakup chips off a tiny granite flake from the rock, and carries it downstream. The flake adds its mite to a pure white sandbar. A hundred more runoffs and the flake is now a rounded grain of sand, moving downward and eastward on an ever-slowing river. Chemical weathering takes over now, loosening the internal bonds of the sand grain, releasing tiny plates only molecules thick. Tumbling slowly, buoyant in a spring flood current, new Rocky Mountain clay moves downstream towards its destination prairie.

Forest is the ultimate sere, the vegetation set that all others aspire to. The living forest self-regulates, needs no consumer or grazer (except perhaps fire) and seems to be an end in itself. Old growth climax forest can become decadent and is subject to blowdowns, fire, disease, and insect infestations. But when these events happen, the scars are not permanent, and the disturbance ultimately diversifies the mosaic of ages and species. In our enthusiasm for forest management we would do well to remind ourselves that these same forests practiced self-management successfully for some 9,000 years.

I can see that fire will be a major question for me. Generations of us were imprinted with the image of Smokey the Bear. The death of Bambi's mother was a recurring childhood trauma, and we grew up instinctively reacting against forest fire. Our government agencies have amassed huge resources and talent to control fire, but evidence is accumulating that fire is an integral and healthy part of many ecosystems. There is even evidence of ancient fires in tropical forests.

The bottom of the Rocky Mountain Trench, from Invermere to Cranbrook, was historically a semi-open, fire-maintained grassland. Tree ring data showed fires occurring on average every 6.9 years. With the advent of effective fire suppression however, tree ingrowth in the Trench has been phenomenal, and much of it is now occupied by dense "doghair" lodgepole pine thickets. These thickets may contain as many as 30,000 stems per hectare and individual trees may only reach a few centimeters in diameter after decades of growth. Yet the sheer denseness of these thickets eliminates all the understory grasses and shrubs. Instead of creating wildlife habitat, an unburned lodgepole thicket creates a virtual vacuum.

Lodgepole pine evolved in the crucible of fire. In fact, the cones of this species, like those of its northern prairie relative, jackpine, must be heated before they will open to release their seed. Lodgepole under normal conditions does not code for a monoculture; it codes for an infinite mosaic of itself and grass.

Older rangemen familiar with the Trench have shown me isolated examples of the original landscape: there are scattered fire-scarred veteran trees, brash young seedlings, a few juveniles, and a rich understory of shrubs, wildflowers and grass. Fire has taken the lower limbs of the veterans, so grass grows right up to their trunks, and there is visibility to medium distance. From my own, human perspective, there is an intuitive correctness about this landscape; it feels right to me. Paleontologists tell us this kind of environment was our cradle, the meeting of forest and grassland, the dynamic edge, the open/closed landscape, the zone of tension, the fire-maintained mosaic.

The personal and property risks of fire are very real, and the modern concerns about carbon dioxide and particulate release into the atmosphere are legitimate. But controlled fire and managed grazing are the most natural means of landscape manipulation available to us. There is an awakening of interest in these two techniques as alternatives to herbicides and heavy metal, which are becoming less and less attractive to our society.

Place-discovery in my new forest landscape means tentative hikes and explorations, looking at other people's slides, asking questions, studying floras, learning the geography and the back roads. Prairie runs out to the horizon and is defined by its grid roads and townships; these forests are marked out by drainage basins and heights of land. On the prairies, precipitation is the dominant landscape variable. In the mountains, elevation becomes dominant.

After fishing isolated mountain trout streams, I like to take my clothes off and slip into them quietly, to drift for a few moments. This is my ritual of landscape orientation. First the cold, transparent water, moving toward the Pacific; then the rounding stones underneath; then molten sun overhead, and finally, western red cedars on right and left flank.

The plant and animal species are a challenge. Every now and then I see an old friend, learned in some other place, and I am grateful for the familiarity. More often I listen open-mouthed to stories of bear, elk and mountain goat, or look dumbly at an unknown wildflower.

As I sat on a rock slab the other day, eating a sandwich, an old familiar species scuttled by and then stopped in front of me, as if he were announcing his Kootenay presence: he was an alligator lizard. Tucked in among the grand sweep of forest organisms, insignificant to the point of being an ecological joke, a Mediterranean species really not belonging here at all, the lizard did a few pushups on the granite, just for show. A flood of herpetological memories came back. Before he rushed off to his next important alligator lizard appointment, I think, no I am sure, he winked at me. His presence suddenly made this great new forest landscape more approachable.

Hubris

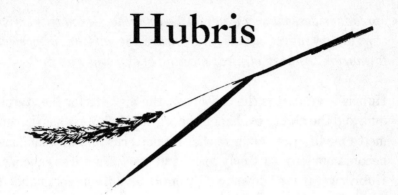

Bright green scum of duckweed on the water surface; August. Willows and dogwoods arch over the main river channel, suspended in the heat. Butcher birds impale frogs on spines of buffalo berry. Oxbow, cutbank and meander form complex riparian signatures. Memories of spring runoff with its ice jams, overflow, siltation, disorder, are distant. This is now the high season of stagnant afternoons, insects, fishkill. Heavy earth on the adjacent floodplain is finally drained and desiccated by the heat. In its dry brush and insurgent weeds the grasshoppers pulse, like migraines.

Or open, confused shores of recent sand. Sheet of water surface clean, like molten lead. Far in distant downriver, a low line of dam looking insignificant. Peaceful, ordered waterscape, abiotic except for introduced perch and desultory waterskier. Siltation proceeds clandestine, submarine. Massive, unprecedented evaporation creates pleasant cumulus overhead. Waterfowl dabble for mud and spent lead shot. Two-cycle slick *spreads iridescent over water by new marina. Gaunt transmission towers march up the hills toward the horizon, in perfect formation. August; clinical meeting of sky and water.*

Hubris is vital. It is the brashness, the distaste for the status quo, and the ability to change the world. My hubris has driven me to modify the earth, so that its patterns and mechanisms become obvious, so I may learn and grow from its response. Hubris was passed down to me from Jehovah, who commanded me to first name the things of the earth, and then:

"fill the earth, and subdue it; and rule over the fish of the sea and over the birds of the sky, and over every living thing that moves on the earth."

I did that.

Dams were truly the apogee of my hubris. I trained self-confident men and put them in arrogant institutions to build dams. I asked them to bring rivers, the wildest, most random and most vital of earth's essences, under my control. They responded magnificently, shackling the Columbia, one of our namesake rivers, with a litany of dams on its 2000 kilometer length: Bonneville, The Dalles, John Day, McNary, Priest Rapids, Rock Island, Rocky Reach, Chief Joseph, Coulee, Keenleyside, Duncan, and Mica. Then they shackled the Columbia's tributaries as well, damming the Deschutes, the Snake, the Pend O'reille, and the Kootenay. They developed Hoover, James Bay, Oldman, and Rafferty on my behalf. I was awash with neutral and objective power, for the industrialization of our landscape. There was nothing these men could not do.

My hubris was unique to western North America: it was my

New World birthright. I thought it was different from all the rest, I thought I could go on this way forever, because of the grandness of my landscape, and my youthful overconfidence. I did a hundred misdeeds to the continent in the name of hubris.

The fine old biblical prescription of conquest worked for a time, since I carried it out in the earth-based context of a rural, agrarian society. My compulsive alterations of the land were balanced by wildness, back country, and the smell of sagebrush after a summer thunderstorm. The buffered natural wealth of North America offered me some 200 years of uncomplicated, exploitative growth. But somehow, imperceptibly, a sea of urban asphalt has now risen around me. Agriculture has been marginalized from my society, and every shiny new surface I manufacture or consume now seems to have some sticky, festering environmental horror underneath.

I have crossed a profound threshold: it is the end of an earth-bonding that develops naturally through a rural, agrarian society, and the beginning of concentrated, excess pollution beyond my earth's ability to absorb, detoxify, and forgive. This may be the biggest event in human history. I have tried to assign a specific date when I crossed that threshold; it could be 1914, with the start of World War I; 1932, the black spring of the prairies; 1967, the breakup of the supertanker *Torrey Canyon*; 1976, the dioxin explosion in Seveso, Italy; 1979, Three Mile Island; 1989, *Exxon Valdez*; 1990, Hagersville, or the approaching year of the Columbia River's thirteenth dam. I haven't yet been able to settle on a single choice. The field of candidate events will no doubt get wider.

Communications about these environmental events are omnivorous, and overwhelming. I learn instantly, in great detail, about all our latest crises, both short and long term. The chemistry of sulfur dioxide in the air of our industrial valleys is painstakingly explained, citing sources, rates and consequences. I hear of the black rain from tillage-based agriculture, and of the brown rivers below the clearcuts. I read about the casual dissemination of heavy metals and radionuclides. I learn a great deal about the massive quantities of atmospheric emissions.

I seek out other information, on herbicide residues, pulp mill effluent, and phosphate loading. I know that fighting good environmental fights is important. Specific policies are important, particularly those dealing with energy and agriculture. My own lifestyle changes to reduce waste are important. I know economics are important, as the 1970s showed me that energy conservation is almost totally price-driven, and the 1990s will show the same for recycling. Good will is important. People like to change, make an effort, when approached in the right way. Governments do, in their own stumbling fashion, have some relevance to the earth, mostly in a negative sense, but I must remember that we always elect the ones that are true expressions of ourselves as a country. I must also remind myself that the frequent numbness and stasis in government bureaucracy has little to do with the party in power, and much to do with the human condition. And I know that four decades of a cheap food policy has wreaked havoc in agriculture, pushing it into unsustainable practices, just so I could buy bread for a dollar.

But these things are all secondary. The biggest problem is that I don't really care.

I have lost a mother; that is the main issue. I glimpse her momentarily in between cities, and perhaps on summer holidays in the back country. But that doesn't sustain me. My natural, societal bond with earth has been broken, and I can never go back to the agrarian conditions that produced it. I have no idea what my earth morals should be, and in the great range of our alterations to this planet, I haven't the sense and the courage to draw the line between the sustainable and the unacceptable. This is the real environmental crisis, the higher logic behind all those specific events; I have somehow willed myself to become an unfeeling urban runaway, an environmental street kid, and I just don't care very much about the fate of the earth. In this frame of mind, all the wealth of environmental information I receive means little.

I know I should care more about what is being done to my earth. Knowing I don't care is enervating and unpleasant. It drives me on to ever more consumptive distractions.

My precious hubris no longer belongs to me. It has become institutionalized, and is the property of those arrogant organizations whose earth context is even more tenuous than mine. As an individual, I mainly watch TV, and wonder occasionally how we arrived at this state.

Sometimes I do get involved, for or against various developments. I join debates on dams, pulp mills, herbicide registrations and jobs. I see less and less of the "fortress mentality" and "compromise" traditional to Canadian political life and more of the American approach of separate, scornful enclaves. The Canadian rednecks and the Canadian greens, the earth-muffins and the earth-eaters, stay more and more apart, meeting now only in courtrooms and picket lines. We avoid each other, requiring the total reinforcement of unanimous thinking. We fear the possibility – horror of horrors – that we might like each other. We fear the possibility that the other person's lifestyle may not be built completely on rural rape, or urban decadence.

But every now and again I see that the morality behind our

collective positions as forced and artificial, a brave front covering the common and profound loss.

Once I had a prescription for the earth bond. It was simple: I watched the sun rise in the morning, and I produced food. The rest followed automatically. Thàt option for my society is now gone, forever, and other means of recreating the earth bond must be found.

There is a balance in all societies between science and myth, reason and the imagination. Mine has its balance profoundly tipped toward the rational; it is not partial to explorations by means of concentrated personal insight and imagination, except within the very traditional and defined disciplines of poetry, painting, or theater. If we are ever to renew our earth bond, a rebalancing must occur. New bonds with the earth can now only be forged by personal explorations that go far beyond simple analysis and concern, into realms of imagination and myth.

* * *

I cannot leave the issue of earth bonding without a practical program, even though the crux of it is personal and spiritual. My proposal has to do with individual restoration of harmed lands and waters.

I am not talking here about beautification, about lawns and flowerbeds, although that has a place. I see individuals adopting bits and pieces of wrecked urban, industrial, agricultural or forest land, analyzing them, beginning a gentle purging of their pollutants, and making a crude attempt to guide these victims back toward their natural successional pathways. This last activity is a conundrum, because a significant part of what we perceive as "natural" is random, and even the most obvious successional pathways are wide and poorly marked. Part of the restoration to a natural state will involve redefining what "natural" really means.

No ownership will be involved in this land restoration. There shall be care and perhaps, ultimately, love, but no ownership. The land could be public domain, or private. The current landlord might not necessarily solicit or even agree to the project. No implementation agency would be created. Individuals would bear all expense. Any say in a parcel's future would be gained through a person's demonstrated care and individual commitment to it.

Through this process the day may come when we as a whole society will turn to an outdated dam somewhere and say: "This project was built for reasons we now see as selfish and short-sighted. We have made the changes to our lives and infrastructures that will allow us to set this stretch of river free." Slowly the concrete will come down, under the watchful eye of less arrogant men and women, less arrogant institutions. Spawning beds, oxbows, and willows will reappear, and we will have returned a small piece of the earth's stolen heirloom.

There is a moving sequence in David Attenborough's film *Gandhi* that relates to this exercise. At the height of the religious carnage following India's independence, Gandhi started a fast to protest the violence in his new country. One night a man came to Gandhi's bedside, a Hindu, who confessed to having murdered a Muslim child in retribution for the violent death of his own son. The man was in an agony of guilt, and asked Gandhi for guidance. "Go and find a child," Gandhi said,

" a male child that has been orphaned by the war, and raise him. But raise him as a Muslim."

Adoption is hubris redefined. It too is a reckless venturing into the unknown, and an overwhelming confidence in one's own abilities to understand and modify. But it also means great sensitivity to ravaged identities, and a sense of stewardship that is broadened from mere parcels to ecosystems, and to continents.

The grand sweep of western Canadian landscape is now before me: prairie, mountain, coulee, badland, floodplain, and outlier. The mechanisms of these places, those that are known to me, pulse reassuringly. The whole landscape is now my dream bed, where I will seek a new relationship with earth, to be influenced by the flows of its nature and, if I am lucky, to spawn a few of its visions.

Chapter
References

Introduction

Berry, Wendell. *The Unsettling of America: Culture and Agriculture.* Sierra Publications, 1986.

Dormaar, John. "Waiting for a Vision." *The Explorer's Journal* 66 (1988): 145-149.

Holton, Gerald. "Constructing a Theory: Einstein's Model." *American Scholar* (1979): 309-340.

Landscape Mathematics

Adams, Ansel. *Photographs of the Southwest.* New York: New York Graphic Society, 1984.

Monthly Temperature Summaries (1981). Atmospheric Environment Service, Winnipeg, Manitoba.

Butler, William. *The Great Lone Land: A Tale of Travel in the North and West of America.* Toronto: Musson Book Co., 1924.

Weaver, J.E. and F.W. Albertson. *The Grasslands of the Great Plains.* Chicago: Johnson & Co., 1956.

In the Heart of the Matter: Phloem Research

Biddulph, Orlin. "The Application of Radioactive Isotopes to Biological Research." *Northwest Science* 221 (1947): 153-156.

Coupland, Robert, ed. *The Grassland Ecosystems of the World.* London: Cambridge University Press, 1979.

Kennedy, J.S. and T.E. Mittler. "A Method for Obtaining Phloem Sap via the Mouth Parts of Aphids." *Nature* 171 (1953): 528.

Small, James. *Practical Botany.* London: J.A. Churchill Ltd., 1931.

Weatherly, P.E. and A. J. Peel. "The Physiology of the Sieve Tube." *Journal of Experimental Botany,* v. 10 (1959).

Deeper into Prairie

Dormaar, John. "Effect of Boulder Flow on Soil Transformation under Teepee Rings." *Plains Anthropologist* 21 (1976): 115-118.

Jenny, Hans. "The Image of Soil in Landscape Art, Old and New." *Pontific Academy Science Scripta* var 32 (1968): 948-979.

Kehoe, Thomas F. *Indian Boulder Effigies*. Regina: Government of Saskatchewan, Museum of Natural History, 1965.

Turner, Frank. *Across the Medicine Line*. Toronto: McClelland and Stewart, 1973.

West, N. and J. Skujins. "The Nitrogen Cycle in North American Coldwinter Semidesert Ecosystems." *Ecologia Plantarum* 12 (1977): 45-53.

Salt of the Earth

Archer, John., in *Furrows and Faith: A History of the Old Wives Township*, 1980.

Bragg Creek, Alberta

Journals of Samuel Hearne and Philip Turnor. (Includes journals of Peter Fidler.) Toronto: J.B. Tyrell, 1934.

Jahn, R.G. and B.J. Dunne. *Margins of Reality: The Role of Consciousness in the Physical World.* New York: Harcourt, Brace, 1987.

Savory, Alan. *Holoistic Resource Management.* Island, California, 1988.

On the Outlier

Gallup, William B. "Plateau of Empire," in Alberta Society of Petroleum Geologists, 15th Annual Field Conference Guidebook, part 1 (1965), 30-36.

Hugh Kortschack, Pineapples, and the C4 Syndrome

Budd, Archibald. *Budd's Flora of the Canadian Prairie Provinces.* Ottawa: Research Branch, Agriculture Canada, 1979.

Haberlandt, Gottfried. *Physiological Plant Anatomy.* Translated by M. Drummond. London: Macmillan, 1884.

Hatch, M.D. and C.R. Slack. "Photosynthsesis by Sugarcane Leaves: A New Carboxylation Reaction and the Pathway of Sugar Formation." *Biochemical Journal* 101 (1966): 103-111.

Harms, Vernon and J.H. Hudson. "Some Vascular Plants New to the Flora of Saskatchewan." *Canadian Field Naturalist* 92 (1978): 389-391.

Kortschack, H.P., et al. "Carbon Dioxide Fixation in Sugarcane Leaves." *Plant Physiology* 49 (1965): 1021-3.

Analogues and Desire

Audobon Society. *Field Guide to North American Fossils.* New York: Knopf, 1981.

Spry, Irene, *Papers of the Palliser Expedition,* 1857-1860. Toronto: The Champlain Society, 1968.

Stegner, Wallace. *Wolf Willow.* Lincoln: University of Nebraska Press, 1980.

Watching the Grass Grow

Gayton, Don. "Leaf Growth and Response to Defoliation in Western Wheatgrass." Master's thesis, University of Saskatchewan, 1974.

Symbiosis

Postgate, J.R. *Fundamentals of Nitrogen Fixation.* London: Cambridge University Press, 1983.

The Grass and the Buffalo

Chisholm, B., et al. "Assessment of Prehistoric Bison Foraging and Movement Patterns via Stable-carbon Isotopic Analysis." *Plains Anthropologist* 1986: 193-204.

Dormaar, J.F., et al. "Long-term Soil Changes Associated with Seeded Stands of Crested Wheatgrass in Southeastern Alberta,Canada." *Proceedings*, First International Rangelands Conference, 1978: 623-25.

Gray, James. *Men Against the Desert*. Saskatoon: Western Producer Prairie Books, 1978.

Lodge, Robert. "Complementary Grazing Systems in the Northern Great Plains." *Journal of Range Management* 23 (1970): 268-271.

Mack, Richard and J. Thompson. "Evolution in Steppe with Few Large, Hooved Animals." *American Midland Naturalist* 119 (1982): 757-773.

Roe, Frank G. *The North American Buffalo: Critical Study of the Species in Its Wild State*. Toronto: University of Toronto Press, 1951.

The Hellbender at the Bottom
of the Dugout .

Stebbins, Robert. *A Field Guide to Western Reptiles and Amphibians.* New York: Houghton Mifflin, 1985.

Koestler, Arthur. *Janus: A Summing Up.* New York: Random House, 1979.

Roy LaMotte's Cows

Rangelands, published six times a year by the Society for Range Management, Denver, Colorado.

Johnston, A. and C.B. Bailey. "Influence of Bovine Saliva on Grass Regrowth in the Greenhousee." *Canadian Journal of Animal Science* 52 (1972),: 573-74.

The Hole in the Glacier

Bryan, Alan, ed. *Early Man in America, From a Circum-Pacific Perspective.* Edmonton: Archaeological Researches International, 1978.

Martin, Paul. "The Discovery of America." *Science* 179 (1973): 969-73.

The Forest Cycle

Fire in Pacific Northwest Ecosystems. Corvallis: Department
of Rangeland Resources, Oregon State University, 1990.

Printed in Canada